BURIED BY TABLE ROCK LAKE

Tales, anecdotes and facts about everything
covered by the lake

Revised Edition

by Tom Koob

Buried By Table Rock Lake

Copyright © 2006 Tom Koob revised 2018 Tom Koob

ISBN# 978-1-4675-7887-5

24039 Box Elder
Shell Knob, MO. 65747

Printed in the United States of America
Litho Printers & Bindery
Cassville, Missouri 65625

Table of Contents

Introduction

While writing my first book, *The History of Fishing Table Rock Lake*, I became interested in what was under the surface of this large, man-made impoundment. I felt it would be enjoyable and hopefully informative to research what was covered when the water piled up behind Table Rock Dam in the late 1950's.

As with all historical research, it is always a challenge to find the ultimate truth about events in the past. Particularly with stories of the oral tradition, tales change with time. Often, certain events and occurrences are related or documented with some inaccuracy. Retellings continue these errors and sometimes add their own.

I have tried hard to verify the stories in this book. Wherever possible, I have attempted to use multiple sources to arrive at the best possible account. Despite these efforts, I am sure that some errors and misrepresentations have crept in.

When I first began this endeavor, I thought I would accumulate a litany of interesting facts and events- and these are indeed a part of this book. I have come to realize though, that the real story is something else. It is the story of a rugged land and rugged people. It is a tale of a somewhat isolated culture thrust into a modern world not necessarily of its own choosing.

I would like to thank my family and friends for their support during this project. Thanks to those who allowed me to quote from their historical writings, the librarians, historians and proof readers who assisted me, and those who shared their wonderful photographs. Most of all, I owe a debt of gratitude and respect to those who so kindly allowed me to interview them personally. It is these first-hand accounts which bring this history to life.

I hope you enjoy these stories and perhaps discover some you have not heard before. And next time you are driving over or boating across the lake, I hope you know a little more about what was Buried By Table Rock Lake.

2018 Revision

I have been pleasantly surprised by the success of Buried By Table Rock Lake. I wrote this book because I was interested in these stories and thought it would be fun to research this area's history. I didn't realize so many others would share my interest and enthusiasm.

It has been over ten years since I first published this work. Over that time, many of the people I interviewed have passed away. I am thankful that I was able to capture some of their stories. Along the way, many others have shared accounts of their own lives with me. I have continued to research the Ozarks long history and learned many new things about this fascinating area.

With this information, I have revised my original work to include new stories, updates, newly discovered photographs and corrections.

I hope readers will enjoy the original content as well as the new material I have added. The more we open our eyes and ears to the living history around us, the more we will know about what is still Buried By Table Rock Lake.

Tom Koob 2018

Chapter 1
Towns and Settlements

Oasis

Although many small towns were affected by Table Rock Lake, there was only one settlement of any significant size destroyed. This village was Oasis. Oasis was situated on the south side of Long Creek across the stream from Goat Hill just outside the mouth of Big Cedar Hollow. The top of Goat Hill is still visible as a small island about one mile north of the Hwy. 86 bridge over the present-day lake.

The site of Oasis was homesteaded by Judge James Bolton "Boat" Rice after the Civil War. At this time, the area was known as Cedar Valley. Mr. Rice's son Frank Rice and Frank's wife Samantha operated a general store in Cedar Valley.

The bottomland of Long Creek provided fertile soil for the growing of wheat, corn, cotton and tobacco. The hills surrounding the turbulent stream were covered with hardwood and pine forest. A three-story mill was constructed from hand-hewn timbers in 1876. In the late 19th century, Frank Rice sought authority to construct a dam across this section of Long Creek. The following quote from a story written by Douglas Mahnkey in <u>The Ozark Mountaineer</u> describes the building of this dam:[1]

> "The license and authority were granted to Frank Rice and the long and difficult task of damming the wild stream began. Much of the information used in this article came to me first hand from A.W. "Dutch" Burnett who was a small boy at the time the dam was built. A.W.'s parents, John and Mary Burnett, were pioneer settlers in the Long Creek Valley.
>
> Giant pines were cut down and timbers were hewn with broadaxes by the mountain men. These timbers measured about one foot square and were about 16 feet long. Some of the timbers were shorter, about 8 feet. The creek bed at the site of the dam was solid rock. The stream was narrow at this point, an

estimated 400 feet. The south side was hemmed in with a high rock ledge and the north by a bluff. The water ran at a fierce speed between these two banks. The work had to be done in summer when the water was at the lowest flow of the season. Strong and solid pens had to be first constructed. Workmen with hand drills and sledge hammers drilled holes at regular intervals in the solid rock in a line across the stream. This was an engineering feat, the laying out of all this work by Frank Rice. Once the holes were drilled in the rock and like size holes in the hewn timbers the work of setting the pens in place began. A steel rod about eight or nine feet long was set in each hole, driven down good and tight. Then the heavy task of matching the holes drilled in the timbers with the upright rods began. Gradually the pens took shape, held in place by the steel rods. Each pen was about 8 feet high, 16 feet long and 8 feet wide. (These figures are estimated from memory of Dutch and myself).

Stone was hauled from the hills and each pen was filled with stone, extending one against the other all away across the stream from the bluff on the north side to the forebay on the south side. Next a series of holes were drilled upstream about ten feet from the pen in a line all the way across the stream. Steel bars or rods were driven in these and allowed to extend about 12 inches above the bedrock of the stream. Holes were bored in hewn timbers to match the upright rods and the timbers fitted in place all the way across the stream. Heavy hewn timbers of pine, about 16 feet long, were then put in place, extending from the line of timbers which had been laid just upstream from the pens and resting on a like line of timbers laid and fastened along the top of the rock-filled pens. When finished, the whole thing looked much like rafters on the framework of a building.

Heavy planks furnished by the local sawmill from pine harvested in the nearby hills were then hauled by wagon and teams to the damsite. Beginning at the stream bed, these planks were laid in place across the rafters the full width of the stream. Spikes were driven to hold the planks in place even though the water pressure would hold them. The men had to work quickly, for the water was being impounded and the mill pond taking form behind them.

While all this was going on, other workmen had been constructing the forebay against the rock cliff on the south side of the creek. This was a big concrete box about 12 feet square extending from the solid rock at the base of the mill dam to a height greater than the dam itself. The upstream side of the square concrete structure was flush with the dam. This housed the turbine. We do not know where the turbine was purchased. This was a great improvement over the old overshot wheels that were used in pioneer mills. An opening was left in the upstream side of the forebay and a huge wooden door was made so it would slip up and down this opening. To operate the turbine the gate was lifted, allowing the water to rush into the forebay and turn the turbine with great speed, by means of a strong lever and rope and chain. This was operated from a little porch on the first floor of the mill building directly above the forebay.

The completed dam backed the waters of Long Creek up for about a quarter mile. The mill pond was a thing of beauty providing a place for boating and swimming as well as skating in the winter time.

The mill dam must have impeded the passage of fish up the stream. We found in the old Circuit Court Records of Taney County Vol. 3 that J.B. Rice had been indicted by a grand jury for "obstructing the passage of fish up Long Creek." The case was on the docket for a long time, being continued from term to term. Finally on Oct. 27th, 1896, the Prosecuting Attorney, Col. R.C. Ford dismissed the case, and it was ordered that Mr. Rice recover his costs. Judge James T. Neville was presiding in the Court at the time. I recall that as late as 1922 people who lived up the creek from the mill dam complained about the fish being blocked. There was a makeshift fish ladder, but I never saw a fish near it."

The presence of the mill helped establish Cedar Valley as a local commerce center. In addition to the mill, there was a general store, a cotton gin, a sawmill, a blacksmith shop, a post office and a few homes. The mill also functioned as a polling place. In addition to the Rice family, the mill was owned over the years by the Wells, Kirkham, Stires, Johnson, Mahnkey, Eychaner and Burnett families. The dam was washed out by a flood in 1927.

Some time in the early 20th century, Cedar Valley was renamed Oasis. It was indeed considered to be a beautiful, watery place among the rough, wild hills. The following quote from *A Candle Within Her Soul* by Ellen Gray Massey describes the scene:[2]

"A row of catalpa trees lined the lane from the store to the large red barn. Willows and other trees formed a narrow border on either side of Long Creek as it made a big bend around the valley to the mill where it turned north to disappear into forested bluffs. A few other buildings, a low, hand-hewn shingled blacksmith shop and two or three other houses, clustered around the store where the road from the east converged with one road that forded the creek to follow it north and another that led south to Blue Eye and on into Arkansas."

People came from miles around to have their grain processed, purchase supplies, pick up mail and vote. Roads from the north, south and east all converged on Oasis. Two fords, Deep Ford and Shallow Ford crossed Long Creek providing access to the community. Prior to 1920, Taney County built a one-lane steel bridge across the stream just below the dam. They were not, however, able to build adequate approaches and the bridge was unused by road traffic for several years. In 1925, the road work was completed and the span became the Route P crossing over Long Creek.

C.P. and Mary Elizabeth Mahnkey purchased the Oasis mill and store in 1922 and operated them until 1935. The Mahnkeys worked hard to make a living and raise their family during these "hard" times. The blacksmith shop and sawmill were operated by C.P.'s brother Bill. The Mahnkeys built and rented out three cabins along the creek to early tourists to the area. One of the cabins was called the "Winnie Bee Cabin", named for their granddaughter Winnie Bee Jones-Wolf. In the following quote from A Candle Within Her Soul, Mary Elizabeth Mahnkey describes the tourist trade:[3]

"We had three little cabins along the creek bank that we could rent to tourists. Since we were in such an out-of-the-way spot, we rented them to the same tourists year after year, for not many people could find them. One young couple came from Tulsa each summer. They were Roy and Mildred. Roy loved to fish, but Mildred would fuss every minute they were there. She didn't like to fish! She didn't like the country! She didn't like anything, not even fresh air, I reckon. She would trail along after Roy, just moaning and groaning. We used to laugh about it, and yet we were sorry for him. Then one summer he didn't come. The next summer, there he was again, and Reggie ran down to help

him get settled in the cabin he always took. Then Reggie came back and said, "Roy has his wife with him, but it isn't Mildred!" Sure enough, he had gotten a divorce from Mildred and married a long-legged young thing that would stride ahead of him on the way to the river and out fish him and all the young fellows in the neighborhood."

Running a general store involved long hours and often introduced the Mahnkeys to interesting people and situations. The following two stories related by Mary Elizabeth in *A Candle Within Her Soul* illustrate life in Oasis:[4]

"One night a poor distracted fellow came and got my husband out of bed to go to the telephone for a doctor, as one was needed and Granny Gibson was across the river at another stork party. The doctor was gone, so we decided that I had better go down, for no one else was there, only another neighbor woman. I ran lightly along the road, not afraid in the deep soft summer darkness, for Rexie, the little dog was with me. Yet horribly frightened too, for this was a crisis, and I did not know what to do. But the sick lady told us what to do. "Take an' git some little peach tree limbs, water sprouts, if'n you can find 'em, take off the outside bark, an' scrape the inside bark down, and make hit into tea." This we did and she drank the bitter brew uncomplainingly. Then I sat down by her bed and talked of many, many things. I even repeated old poems, and directly she fell asleep and slept sweetly till daylight and the arrival of gallant old Granny Gibson. My husband said he always knew that I was a fluent talker, but this was the first time any one had ever out talked the old stork in his determination. Yet sometimes I shudder to think what might have been if the peach tree twigs had been scraped the wrong way."

"Once when she was alone in her upstairs lookout, she spotted a car coming, much bigger and finer than any in the country at that time. The motor was so quiet she would have missed it if she hadn't been looking right at it. The driver, a large, handsome well-dressed man with his hat pulled down over his eyes, stopped down the road a short distance, left the motor running, and ran into the store.

"I need some groceries and I'm in a great hurry," he panted. "You don't mind if I help you pack them up?"

Mary Elizabeth got a big cardboard box as he began grabbing items off the shelves, saying, "Tomatoes! Salmon! Pork and Beans! Crackers! Corn!"

When they had the box full, he took out a billfold and thumbed through the bills. She tried not to stare at the hundred and five hundred dollar bills. Sorting through the bundle, he pulled out a fifty dollar bill.

Mary Elizabeth looked at it, "I don't believe I can change that!" She lied. She didn't want to unlock the post office money while alone with him.

"I must have some change." He looked down at her frightened expression and added in a kind, reassuring voice, "Mother, I wouldn't harm a hair of your head."

She walked to the post office. Her hand did not tremble on the hard combination as she unlocked the money. She knew the man had harmed others, but she also knew he would not harm her. She counted out the change. No one in the country saw the fellow again. Believing that he was heading for a hide-out in the hills, Mary Elizabeth was glad he bought good substantial groceries."

The Mahnkey's general store at Oasis 1930

The Mahnkey's daughter Bertie taught school at nearby Brush Creek. Their son Douglas taught at Cedar Valley School. Douglas served as Taney County Clerk for four terms and was elected to the Missouri House of Representatives in 1934. Douglas Mahnkey practiced law from Forsyth, Mo. until his recent death in 2004. He wrote extensively about his life and the area in Bright Glowed My Hills and other publications.

Mary Elizabeth Mahnkey was a prolific writer of poems, stories and articles. Her insightful understanding of real people and life in the Ozarks shines through her work. Her writings introduced many Americans to the beauty and mystery of these hills and helped found the Taneyhills Library in Branson.

By 1934, the Mahnkeys were struggling with the Depression, their advancing age and the relocation of their children and grandchildren. Talk of damming the White River had been circulating since the early 1900's and by 1934, Table Rock Lake appeared to be inevitable. Concerned about declining property values, the Mahnkeys sold their Oasis property to Bill Eychaner in 1935 for $5000.

It would be several more years before Table Rock Lake would bury the little town of Oasis. But in 1957, when the lake prematurely filled from torrential rains, the beautiful little settlement along with the sturdy mill, several other buildings and the one-lane steel bridge were all buried beneath the rising water.

Now as you cross the modern steel span on Hwy. 86 over Long Creek, perhaps you can visualize this oasis in a wild land. The tiny island marks the hill behind the town and the larger island, the top of Goat Hill which rose prominently above Cedar Valley on the bluff above the surging flow of Long Creek.

Radical

The settlement of Radical is often improperly located on area maps as being on the south side of the White River. The village was generally located on the north side and depending on the whims of the Postal Service, operated near the river or on the ridges well above the White. The 1930 Stone County Plat Map places Radical southwest of the Kimberling Crossing very near the James River. Nelson Holt, longtime postmaster at Reeds Spring, says the Radical post office of the 1930-40's was north of the river, off what is today Joe Bald Road. Mr. Holt confirms that postmaster positions were often awarded based on a political patronage system. New postmasters would sometimes move their office to a new location, close to their home or business, but retain the office name. This accounts for places like Radical being in different locations during different time periods. Nelson Holt says he doesn't believe Radical was ever south of the White River.

Radical existed first as Mayberry (or Mabry), a stopping place on the Wilderness Road. Fording the river was a necessary, but dangerous task. During high water, travelers might have to wait for several days to cross the White. The highland above the river became a temporary campsite. Possibly as early as 1847, a ferry operated at this location. The Mayberry family and others operated a ferry here until 1870.

In 1868, William Wesley Kimberling lived on property on the north side of the White and operated a store out of his home. He also served as postmaster for the village known as Mayberry. Kimberling and Henry Thomas purchased the Mayberry ferry in 1870. The ferry was old, so they built a new one. The gunnels on the new ferry were 42 feet long, each consisting of two pieces spliced together. The ferry ran on a steel cable with the current providing the force to cross. The Kimberling ferry operated upstream of the site of the present-day bridge until 1922.

In 1874, Kimberling purchased land and moved his home to the south side of the White. The Federal government did not want to move the post office to what they considered a less accessible site, so they sent a Federal representative to the area to investigate the post office location situation. Sam Stewart, W.W. Kimberling's son-in-law, applied to be the permanent postmaster at the site on the north shore. The government man and Stewart had a spirited conversation about the post office. Ultimately, the government representative is purported to have stated, "You're the durndest radical man I ever heard of. By golly we will call the post office 'Radical', for you are to be the postmaster, so we will just call that post office Radical."

Radical remained a stopping point on the main north-south route crossing the upper White for decades. In 1922, the Kimberling Bridge was erected on Hwy. 43 crossing the river below Radical.

The bridge was washed out by a flood in April of 1927. The Crane Chronicle reported, "Witnesses who saw the bridge go out said the heavy steel girders floated and bobbed up in the stream like they were of wood, then disappeared from view. It was considered remarkable that the heavy girders did not quickly sink from sight, but the flood water was of such force that they were carried away. About half of the bridge was washed some 300 yards down the river and a great deal of the long approach was also washed out." The bridge was rebuilt by December 1927 reconnecting the populace on either side of the White.

Radical was also a major stopping place during the float fishing era. Many of the float trips from Galena down the James and from Eagle Rock or Shell Knob down the White stopped at Radical for supplies or overnight camping. This float stop was called Camp Thomas. A camp on the south side of the White at Kimberling Crossing was called Kimberling Park.

Bill Rogers ran float trips on the James and White. He operated a motel and fishing camp on the south bank at the Kimberling Crossing. When Table Rock came in, he moved the Bill Rogers Motel to Galena and continued his float service for several years.

Otto Ernest Rayburn lived in the Ozarks and studied its history and folk culture for several years. In 1922-23, Rayburn resided in a shanty he called Hideaway Lodge near the Kimberling Crossing. He taught school, took float trips down the James and White, and hobnobbed with the local residents. In his book, Forty Years in the Ozarks[5], Rayburn described his experiences in the community. He mentions two general stores just up Fisher Creek owned by Turner and Hammers. The Turner-Kimberling Community and a tent city called "Ragtown" grew up where the new bridge was being built over the White.

Rayburn described life at the river community:

> *"A tent city called "Ragtown" grew up on the hillside and a motley population drifted in. One of the most interesting characters that made his appearance during the boom days was a genial Irishman from somewhere up north. He probably had been a carnival man for he brought a doll rack and a few ragged baseballs with him. He didn't set up his rack in Ragtown, but located it on an island in White River at the mouth of a little creek about three miles from the bridge. He apparently was*

interested in the tourist trade and the only tourists at that time were fishermen floating down the James and White Rivers from Galena to Branson.

I never visited the spot, but neighbors said the Irishman set up his doll rack on the island near the water's edge where he could hail the fishermen as they approached. 'Stop and have a little fun, boys. Knock the babies off the rack. Three balls for a quarter of a dollar and three down gives you a ticket to joyland.' Such a strange invitation aroused the curiosity of the fishermen and many of them stopped to see what is was all about. Not many of them knocked three in a row, for it was a difficult feat, but it is alleged that they usually left the island with a jug (contents unknown) in their possession."

"On one Fourth of July we had a picnic in the Fisher Creek Valley near the two stores and I helped Hammers operate a lemonade stand. There were two dance platforms on the grounds and plenty of moonshine likker to keep things lively. "Little George" Baize was one of the fiddlers and he knew how to get music out of a fiddle. The most exciting event at this picnic was when the boys had a battle royal with Roman candles. I sold out our entire stock of fireworks in a matter of minutes after the fight started. The crowd scattered like a flock of quail in a barrage, taking refuge behind trees and rocks to escape the fire. No one was injured seriously, but a few of the boys got their shirts burned full of holes.

On another July 4th a group of families had a picnic on the south bank of White River near where the bridge was being built. After dinner some of the men got liquored-up and decided to go swimming. The river was up and one fellow attempted to swim the stream. When he hit the strong current about half way across he realized that he could not make it and called for help. George Hammers went to his rescue, but could not save him. The man drowned almost directly under the partially constructed bridge. A crowd collected and a party was organized by George Turner to recover the body. They tested the current with floating objects to determine its direction and used gigs to locate the body. After about an hour it was found and divers brought it to the surface. This Independence Day had a sad ending in the Turner-Kimberling community."

"Kimberling's Ferry was still in use in 1922 and one day, in November, a shoe drummer, driving a Model T Ford, stopped at Hammers' store. Leaving the store he drove to the ferry which was a whoop and a holler down the lane. The river was high, the

12

approach slick and treacherous, and Mr. Kimberling advised
against crossing. But the salesman wanted to get to Eureka
Springs to spend the night at the Basin Park Hotel so he headed
his Ford down the embankment. He hit the ferry all right but
the brakes of his car did not hold and it skidded into the river
which was twenty feet deep at that point. The salesman escaped
from the car, swam to the ferry, and hurried to the store to get a
change of clothing. A team of mules was secured to drag the car
from the river. George Hammers was one of the best swimmers
in the vicinity and the drummer gave him $10 to dive into the
cold water and tie a rope to the axle. The accident happened
about noon and it was almost sundown before the salesman was
on his way to Eureka Springs. He lost most of his shoes from
the open car and many of them were picked up later by natives
in drifts and eddies down the river. But it did not do them any
good. Sample shoes are all for the same foot."

Rayburn only mentioned Radical once in his book saying, "The southern part of Stone County, Missouri, down Radical way, was all hustle and bustle during the year 1922."[6] This adds to the evidence that Radical was not at the Kimberling Crossing, at least in the years Rayburn was there. Nevertheless, the name Radical continued to be used, showing up on maps as late as 1944.[7]

John Q. Hammons of Springfield purchased land around the Kimberling Crossing anticipating the development of Table Rock. He registered the name Kimberling City in 1959 and built the Kimberling Inn on the high bluff above the river. It is fitting that Kimberling City preserves the name of the family that contributed so much to the history of this site. Hammons foresaw the great potential of this major crossing point. What had existed as a hunting camp, a pioneer settlement and a float fishing stop is now a prosperous resort community.

Above the lake, there is little indication of the history that occurred here. Below the lake lie the site of the Wilderness Road and the Kimberling Ferry. The old Kimberling Bridge still lies nearly completely intact where it once braced against the flow of the White River. Now over a hundred feet below the lake's surface, the bridge slowly erodes, a home for fish.

Beaver

For centuries, native peoples partook of the healing springs near what would become Eureka Springs. They hunted and gathered along the small streams running into the great White. In the early 1800's white settlers began moving up the White and its tributaries. In 1846, John Gaskin built a log cabin on the shoulder of Basin Mountain above Leatherwood Creek. (Part of this original cabin is now Gaskin's Restaurant.)

Leatherwood Creek Valley created a natural path that would be used by Civil War soldiers, bushwackers and farmers. In the 1880's, the first railroad was built along Leatherwood to reach Eureka Springs. The roadbed for the tracks followed the creek until it reached Cedar Bluff, a high, narrow ridge called the Narrows separating the creek and the White River. To extend the railroad it was necessary to cut a large, v-shaped notch through the rocky bluff and build a trestle bridge across the White to Beaver. Eventually, the North Arkansas Railway followed this same route passing by the Elk Ranch and near Brooklyn, the site of a significant limestone quarry.

Off to the north, lay the large peninsula created by Leatherwood Creek and the winding White River. The peninsula has had many owners and names over the years. The Bandys homesteaded the land in the 1850's and called it "The Bottom Place" and later "Bandy's Bend". In 1868, the Burnetts named it "The Homestead Place". In 1938, Richard Shields purchased the property and built "Palisades Farm", a ranch for thoroughbred horses. Henry Banach bought the ranch in 1954 and promoted it as a "fisherman's paradise" resort. The McCullough Corporation purchased the "island" and considerable surrounding acreage in 1970 and developed the present Holiday Island Community.

Well before the railroad came, the hamlet of Beaver Town on the upper White in Arkansas was originally known as Rector's Place. Wilson Beaver established a ferry at the site in the 1850's and the location became known as Beaver's Ferry. Mr. Beaver built a house, stagecoach inn and grist mill on the shores of the White. One can imagine the harrowing ride in a wagon or stagecoach along the rough trail leading to the river, pulling onto the wooden ferry and being carried across the water by the river's current.

Wilson Beaver was the first postmaster with the town being officially named Beaver in 1881. The town was a popular destination for visitors from Eureka Springs. The North Arkansas Railroad eventually crossed the White at Beaver and contributed significantly to the town's growth.

A general store was built with limestone blocks by Mark Swope at Beaver on the banks of the White in 1901. This structure still stands today. Next door, the Riverside Inn once provided accommodations and chicken dinners to guests. The Inn is gone now, but the solid general store still stands as a testament to the ruggedness of the building material and the people who built it.

In 1926, Carroll County constructed a wooden trestle automobile bridge at Beaver. This bridge led people to the town until it was destroyed by a flood in 1943. To alleviate the isolation brought about by the loss of the bridge, the county solicited bids for a new suspension bridge in 1944. The Little Golden Gate Bridge was built by Pioneer Construction Company between 1947 and 1949. During construction, the span was raised 40 feet and lengthened to accommodate the Corps of Engineers plans for Table Rock Lake. This impressive structure, providing an impressive and exciting approach to Beaver Town, is on the National Register of Historic Places. Recently, the suspension bridge has survived overtopping by record high water levels on Table Rock Lake.

The railroad through Beaver discontinued service in 1961. The rail lines were used for a time in the 1970's and 80's as an excursion railroad out of Eureka Springs. Beaver was incorporated in 1949, but had no acting government until a re-incorporation in 1980.

The filling of Table Rock Lake raised the normal water level at Beaver only slightly. The original Corps Park at Beaver was slated for closure in 1980. The town made arrangements to lease the property and now operates the campground at Beaver Park.

Beaver store today

The river at Beaver is probably about as close to original river conditions as exist on the upper White. Of course, the flow is greatly modified by releases from Beaver Dam about ten miles upstream. Fluctuations in Table Rock's level affect water depth at the site. The water leaving Beaver Lake is much colder than the original river. These conditions have created an excellent environment for trout. The Arkansas Game & Fish Commission has stocked rainbow, brown, brook and cutthroat trout into this portion of the White River.

Perhaps when crossing the one-lane suspension bridge or trolling down the lake for trout at this point, you can imagine a stagecoach careening down the grade toward the ford or visualize a railroad car loaded with passengers crossing the old rail bridge over the White River at Beaver Town.

Golden Gate Bridge at Beaver

16

Cape Fair

The wooded ridges, grassy terraces and cane flats where Flat Creek pours into the James River were originally a campsite for Osage Indians. The area was visited by James Yoachum in 1790. On Christmas Day 1835, the John B. Williams, Zachariah Henson and Elijah Todd families arrived in their wagons at the mouth of Flat Creek. One legend says that when these tired pioneers arrived at their destination, they looked back over the steep, rugged trail they had been following. The sight of the perilous path behind them caused them to dub their vantage point Cape Fear.

Another story says these early travelers had arranged for Delaware Indian guides when they reached the upper James River. When the pioneer group arrived at the spot where Flat Creek flowed into the James, they asked their guides what this site was called. The words the Delaware used to describe the location translated "perfect cape' or "fair cape" or "cape fair".

A third and popular theory has the Williams, Henson and Todd group arriving with their Delaware guides and viewing the two streams running together from a high hill. A young man and woman in the party had become sweethearts during the long journey. The beauty of the vista spread out before them caused the young girl to exclaim, "Why, it's a perfect cape!"

A settlement called Jamestown developed at the site with a sawmill, gristmill, blacksmith shop, distillery, cotton gin and general store. The first gunpowder mill west of the Mississippi was built by John Williams at Jamestown. Saltpeter was supplied from bat guano collected from Bear Den Cave just downriver. Joy L. Jones of Cape Fair relates, "When I was growing up, one of the favorite swimming holes for the local kids was at the "big rocks" at Flat Creek. Just below this pool in the creek was the rapids that still contained wooden parts of the mill base."

A tremendous flood destroyed the town in 1844, but the village was rebuilt and a post office was founded here in 1847. In 1851, when Stone County was formed, the first Circuit Court was held in Jamestown at the home of John Williams, but by 1855, Galena had become the county seat.

When the site was flooded again in 1884, the discouraged townfolk decided to move their town to higher ground and the name Cape Fair was resurrected. Silas Carr and William Webster helped plat the new location for Cape Fair. The plat showed streets named Webster, Carr, Wyatt, Main and South.

William T. Stone, a pioneer judge of Taney County, for whom Stone County is named, settled on James River opposite the mouth of Flat Creek around 1840. The large, gentle rise above the curve of the river created an ideal farmstead. The land down by the river became known as Stone Bottoms and the stream crossing, Lower Stone Ford. William Stone built a walnut log cabin on the property and earned a reputation as a skilled farmer and hunter. He planted a large orchard of peach trees which is the probable name source for Peach Orchard Creek, bordering the Stone homestead on the south. Portions of this site above Table Rock Lake are still owned by the Stone family.[8]

Table Rock Lake covered any remnants of Jamestown, but Cape Fair has prospered as a fishing mecca on the large reservoir.

Cape Fair early 20th century

Eagle Rock/Golden

Eagle Rock was first settled in the 1840-50's. It was a natural stop along the trails leading from the White River up Roaring River to its source at the spring. Eagle Rock developed from the proximity of the Easley crossing over White River at the mouth of Roaring River. According to <u>Our Easleys</u>[9], the first post office at Eagle Rock was established in 1854 and called Roaring River. The name of the post office was changed to Eagle Rock in 1886.

The settlement developed on the banks of Roaring River about three miles above White River. In 1868, the Roaring River Baptist Church was organized in a log building. By 1910, R.W. Whittington had a store and post office in a stone building at the village. Whittington is also credited for the grist mill operated just downstream. Roaring River was blocked with a rock and concrete dam creating a mill pond (remnants of this dam are still visible just north of Eagle Rock). In the 1930's, the mill ran a generator that supplied electricity to the store, church and school at Eagle Rock.

The mill and pond were a popular gathering place for local residents who came to have grain ground, purchase supplies and socialize. On special occasions like the Fourth of July, there were celebrations at the mill with baseball games, dancing, rides for children, lemonade and soda pop, and a picnic basket dinner. <u>The Cassville Republican</u> reported on July 7, 1892:

"Eagle Rock News: The celebration at this place was a success. The crowd began to gather at an early hour and by 10 o'clock the grounds were crowded with people. At 10:30 there was a balloon ascension which was a curiosity to the little folks. At 11 o'clock the crowd was called together by singing by the choir. The Declaration of Independence was read by F. M. Bare in his usual pleasant style. The principal oration of the day was made by L. Beasley who caused the eagle to scream and the flag to wave in the usual manner. This was followed by Tennessee Dunlap with a few remarks on the grievances of the American people. But the crowning event was the arrival at a later hour after the committee had concluded he was not coming of Mr.

H. Johnson of Oklahoma who delivered his oration in fine style to the amusement of the best crowd of the day. The fireworks at night were a beautiful sight and a delight to the children. Everything passed off quietly and taken in all, there was never a finer celebration, or a more patriotic people than the people of Eagle Rock, Roaring River township and vicinity."

Noel Curry purchased the Whittington Store in 1925. When Table Rock Lake began filling, the Currys built a new store on higher ground. Jean Curry served as postmistress at Eagle Rock from 1925 until her mandatory retirement in 1971.

"When Curry started in the merchandise business he hauled goods for his store with a team and wagon. He would leave at 4 a.m., drive to Cassville and get home about 8 p.m. He had to ford Roaring River 14 times before he got to the state park site, about half way to Cassville."[10]

The Curry and Taggart stores in Eagle Rock were the centers of the community along with the school and the Baptist Church. The main road through the area, a gravel highway P, crossed Roaring River next to the stores. When the river ran high, the stream could be crossed on a swinging pedestrian bridge.

Lida Wilson Phyles wrote of activities occurring in Eagle Rock in the early 1900's:[11]

"At the old blacksmith shop there was usually a gathering, ready to pitch horse shoes at a moment's notice. The shoes used in the game were kept hanging on the edge of a nail keg in the shop. Cap Bradford saw to it that they were always there. If he did not keep shoes for the purpose, he very often found that shoes he had recently fitted up for some farmer's horse had been carried out without his permission and when the time came to shoe the horse the shoes were otherwise engaged.

The Horseshoe game attracted lots of spectators who stood around, cheered the winners and razzed the losers. They knew that when Henry Skelton, Bill Couch, Finas Ball, and Tinker Wilson were engaged in a hot game there was fun in store for all. Many old timers today recall Tinker Wilson dancing a jubilant jig around a post after he had thrown a ringer."

With the coming of the lake, the new highway and bridge crossing Roaring River at Eagle Rock forced the village farther above the riverbank. Lake development has arranged Eagle Rock along new Highway 86 between the courses of the White and Roaring Rivers.

Dam at Eagle Rock

East of Eagle Rock, the land between the Kings and White has fairly good soil by Ozarks standards. This attractive area was called Hickum Prairie for Robert Hickum who settled here in 1828. The area continued to attract farming interest through the nineteenth century. Grist mills operated on Owl Creek which runs through the area.

After the Civil War, John Leland established a trading post and post office at Golden Ford near Rock Creek on the White. Later, Pilkerton operated the Golden Ferry, one of the early ferries on the White River. In the high meadows of Hickum Prairie at elevation 1163, streams begin and flow in all directions. At this point, the small village of Golden developed.

By the turn of the century, Golden boasted three large general stores, a drug store, post office and barber shop, two churches, a school and several residences. In April 1909, a tornado destroyed much of the town and killed eight people.

Nearly every building in Golden was destroyed including Roberts' store, Henson's store, Dr. Quinn's pharmacy, the blacksmith shop, the Christian and Baptist Churches and the school. Fortunately, school had been dismissed about twenty minutes before the tornado arrived, probably saving the lives of many children. Many homes in and near Golden were demolished or seriously damaged.

After the storm, farming continued to prosper on Hickum Prairie, but the little town struggled to rebuild. Development improved with construction of the Golden Bridge, a two-lane steel span, in 1929 and improvement of the main road Hwy. 39 in 1936. In the 1930's, Golden still had a post office, general stores run by Bud Cope and T.H. Weddington and the Baptist Church. In 1938, the rock schoolhouse was built as a WPA (Works Projects Administration) project. (This rock structure still serves as a library and community building.) In 1940, electricity came to the area with REA (Rural Electrification Administration).

When the Table Rock Project began, no bridge replacement was planned at Golden. Local residents lobbied for a new bridge, but with the approval of the span at Shell Knob, their efforts did not succeed. Golden is now just a small community surrounded by cattle farms and developments along the lake.

Keith Shumaker's grandfather came to the Golden area about 1912 and purchased a large tract of land in Hickum Prairie. Mr. Shumaker drove sheep to his farm from the railhead at Exeter. He also ran cattle and Angora goats on the land he had cleared by hand.

Keith Shumaker grew up on the farm his grandfather had started. He remembers how rough it was traveling on the gravel of Hwy. 39 down to the two-lane steel Golden Bridge. Keith left the Ozarks for a while, but eventually returned and started a successful tire business in Golden.

When asked about how Table Rock Lake affected this area, he says, "There's some things that're worse, but there's a lot of things better. I wouldn't be here if it hadn't been for the lake. I couldn't have made a good enough living."

Shell Knob was first established as a homestead and possibly a trading post by Henry and Elizabeth (Yocum) Schell in 1835. They settled near the base of a large mountain (Shell Knob Mountain) on the White River and stayed in the area until 1845. The area grew slowly with farms established along the river bottomlands and high ridges where the Kings and White Rivers meet.

A little town grew up along the farm-to-market trail north of the river. Jack Carney operated a store at Shell Knob. In 1869, Carney's store was robbed and he and his young wife Cordelia were murdered. When a post office was formed at Shell Knob in 1872, the "c" was dropped from the name. By 1882, the village had forty residents, a public school and a Christian Society church building. Reverend D.W. Gray was the postmaster, Perry Epperly the blacksmith and Drs. Lankford and Maxwell the local physicians.

In the early 20th century, Shell Knob was a thriving market town with the Whisman, Cope and Epperly general stores. Development of Hwy. 86 through Shell Knob in 1933 aided the town's growth. People traveled to the town near the two rivers to take advantage of the fishing and to float the streams. Small vacation homes and "sportsmen" cabins went up around the bridge crossing the White at Shell Knob.

In the early days, the White River was forded just below the mouth of the Kings at Morris Ford. Later, ferries would be operated here by Morris, Fancher and Prentice. In the mid-1800's, there was a settlement known as Jacksonville on the south side of the White near what is today Lost Hill Island. The crossings at this location ended on the north side at Epperly Bluff, named for the Epperly family, longtime residents and landowners in the Shell Knob area. Once on the north shore, a road continued along Mill Creek. This road would eventually become Highway 86 before the building of Table Rock Lake.

The narrow peninsula between Mill Creek and the White River took the name Needle's Eye from a nearby, unusual rock formation with a hole through it. When Table Rock was developed, surveys indicated Epperly Bluff would become an island when the lake level topped the narrow strip of land leading to the peninsula. When the Corps of Engineers develops a project like Table Rock, they are required to purchase all the land within the project's boundaries. Several cabins and homes existed on this property prior to the Project's inception, including the Riverside Park development. To avoid having to purchase all the land and homes at this site, the Corps opted to construct a causeway leading to the peninsula. Many of these homes remain to this day. The portion that would have become an island covers about 70 acres. The configuration of the long, narrow causeway capped by a wider point has upheld the descriptive name Needle's Eye.

A ferry also operated on the White about a mile below the Kings River. Henry Schreiner bought the old Morris split-log ferry in the late nineteenth century. Henry ran a cable ferry service across the White River very close to the present site of the Shell Knob Bridge. The Schreiners (different spellings are used) had a homestead on the south bank of the White about two miles east of the Kings River (this site is now the location of Knob Hill Acres). The Schreiners had a log home on the high terrace above the river. In 1927, they built a new home farther up the hill. The Schreiner place adjoined land owned by the Hardman family. Hardman Cave was located on the south bank of the White.

A rough wagon trail traveled along what is now 39 Highway to the Schreiner place. The ferry road ran down a draw and along Hidden Cove (modern name) out to the river. The Schreiner cable ferry crossed the White depositing passengers on the north shore where the trail ran up High Dive and on to Shell Knob. High Dive took its name from the steep bluff rising above the river at this site.

On July 4, 1935, CCC (Civilian Conservation Corps) Camp #3753 was established at the base of Shell Knob Mountain. The camp generally had about 175 young men, many from surrounding communities, stationed at this location. The CCC boys built an extensive compound and went to work improving the countryside. Some of the accomplishments of the Shell Knob CCC camp include: planted 2.5 million tree seedlings, fought 620 forest fires, helped build five fire towers (Wilderness at Lampe, Sugar Camp, Lohmer, Piney and Shell Knob on top of Shell Knob Mountain), stocked bass into White River, surveyed and constructed fourteen miles of road and improved others including what is today 39-1 and Sugar Camp Road, and installed telephone poles and lines in the region. For several years, the CCC Camp had the only telephone available in Shell Knob. The camp was closed in 1941, but effects of the hard work of the CCC boys can still be seen and appreciated in and near Shell Knob.[12] The site of Camp #3753 is now a community park owned by the U.S. Forest Service and maintained by the Shell Knob Lions Club.

Table Rock Lake forced the relocation and renaming of the roads and the loss of the White River Bridge. Fortunately for Shell Knob, the Central Crossing Bridge was added late in the Table Rock Project process. It is this bridge that has spurred the growth of Shell Knob as a vacation and retirement center.

In the 1800's, the village of Viola experienced development similar to Shell Knob. The Viola post office was founded in 1874 with Isaac Johnson as the first postmaster. The office was discontinued in 1875 and then reestablished in 1880 with postmaster David Plank. In 1893, the Viola post office was relocated to the Barry County side of the village.

By the early 1900's, Viola had its own school, two churches and a physician. There was a general store, gas station and a millinery shop. As in many areas around the White River, farms near Viola grew corn and raised livestock. Cotton and tomatoes were valuable cash crops. In the early 20th century, there was a large steam-powered grist mill in Viola. The mill ground corn and wheat and served as a cotton gin. A tomato canning factory operated in Viola for a time.

The towns of Shell Knob and Viola have had a close relationship for decades. The redefinition of the areal landscape by Table Rock shifted the business life of the vicinity toward

Shell Knob. Viola lost its post office in 1959 after the completion of Table Rock Lake.

Like other small villages of the upper White River area, Viola retains some identity through its inclusion in lake activity and development.

McKee Store at Viola

Baxter/Lampe

In prehistory, the area where Little and Big Indian Creeks flow into the White River was a natural attraction for habitation. There are tales that Spanish explorers spent some time at Breadtray Mountain during DeSoto's trips through the region in the sixteenth century. During the pioneer settlement period, many small towns grew up south of the White River.

Baxter became a primary community between the Wilderness Road and the Kings River. A post office was established at Baxter in 1887. The town had a blacksmith, the Jones School, a saloon and stores run by the Scott and Chappell families.

Edna Hazel McCullough described some of the inventory carried by the store in Baxter in *The History of Stone County Missouri:*[13]

"Available for purchase at these small stores were kerosene, lamps, lamp chimneys and wicks, candy and chewing gum, coffee, sugar, thread, dress goods, salt for man and beast, patent medicines, horseshoes, nails, paper, pencils, ink, envelopes, small gift items at Christmas time, handkerchiefs, bandanas, straw hats, tin cups, milk pails, water buckets, well buckets, rope, binder twine, ice, pop, crackers, slates and slate

26

pencils, axle grease, and after the advent of the automobile, gasoline, seeds, furs, etc.

In turn, the merchant purchased of his customers eggs, cream, sometimes butter which had been molded into one-half and one-pound molds, chickens, turkeys, or other produce which he in turn sold in larger cities. It was largely a barter system, and often time the merchant was left holding the bag!

For shoes, overalls, winter coats, and other items not in stock at the general store, there were the mail order companies which sent the orders out by parcel post. Beyond doubt, this was one of the most useful services ever devised by merchandising. It was made possible by the development of an efficient postal system."

Up Big Indian was the McCullough School which was reached by a swinging pedestrian bridge. Northwest of Baxter, the little town of Earl had a post office from around 1912-1921. Earl was destroyed by a tornado around 1918.

About a mile northeast of Baxter, the flat top of Breadtray Mountain rises to 1347 feet above sea level. The mount's name was applied by early settlers in reference to its rectangular shape and flattened summit. Many legends have been recounted about Breadtray Mountain. Most involve some combination of a silver mine, Indians and Spanish explorers. Otto Rayburn reveals one of these tales in his 1965 "Ozark Guide Yearbook":[14]

"Another legend says that an Indian village was located on the top of Breadtray Mountain. The tribe was haunted by starvation and ill fortune. One day a beautiful girl from a neighboring tribe came to them with the startling information that the Great Spirit would bring them peace and plenty if she became the bride of the chief's son. The wedding took place and the tribe's misfortunes came to an end. The girl was greatly respected by everyone except the medicine man who had profited by the people's misfortunes. He cursed the young woman and she immediately left the village, saying that the Great Spirit would banish the tribe from the face of the earth. Legend says this prediction was carried out and that the curse even extended to the land on the top of Breadtray Mountain. That is the reason nothing grows on the top of the mountain to this day."

East of Baxter, over Black Oak Ridge, the village of Lampe grew up where old Highway 86, constructed in 1933, intersected old Highway 43 (once the Wilderness Road) and ran down to the White. In 1939, the Baxter post office was moved to Baxter Junction on Highway 43 (now 13) and named Lampe in honor of Fayette Lampe, a Springfieldian who owned land in the area.

Baxter, possibly one of the earliest places visited by white men in the Ozarks, is now visited by many vacationers and local residents as the location of the Baxter Marina and Park.

Goodwin Store at Lampe

Nauvoo

South of Baxter near the headwaters of Big Indian Creek, the small town of Nauvoo once existed, just north of the Arkansas state line. Nauvoo is a Hebrew word meaning "beautiful location". The 1927 Stone County Booklet described this town in "beautiful" terms as follows:

"Nauvoo is a pretty rural village in the southwest part of the county located on high land overlooking the Big Indian

28

Creek of clear sparkling water and surrounding farms. It has a county road leading to Missouri Highway No. 43 and to Arkansas Highway 21. Nauvoo has a good rural school and a community of congenial, hospitable and industrious people who welcome all industrious reciprocal homeseekers. Parts of the land is very fertile and all of it is fine for tame grass pastures, tomatoes, small fruits and vegetables. Businesses: J.H. Cule, Postmaster and Merchant; Martin Bilyeu, General Merchandise; Mr. and Mrs. Geo. A. Edwards, General Merchandise; H.E. Freeman, Blacksmith and Corn Mill."

Nauvoo, Illinois was established in 1839 by Joseph Smith as the Illinois headquarters of the Morman Church. Stanley Kimball describes a possible connection between the Illinois and the Missouri Nauvoos: [15]

"There is a local story... to the effect that in the 1890's a James Lawrence visited Nauvoo, Illinois, and upon his return home, named the new post office in his area after Nauvoo, Illinois. This tradition is confirmed by postal documents in the National Archives in Washington, D.C., which show that a post office was established here December 20, 1895, and that the first postmaster was James J. Lawrence."

Today, there is little left of Nauvoo. It is off the main road and mostly forgotten. A stone house and the remains of an old store mark the general vicinity in a peaceful setting.

The old stone house at Nauvoo today

Galena

When Henry Rowe Schoolcraft traversed the White River region in 1818-1819, scouting the area for mineral deposits, he described the area in glowing terms. He camped along the James about six miles from the Finley River near what would become the site of Galena.

> *"We forded the river on horseback, and pursuing up its western bank about four miles, encamped near the shore, in the vicinity of a lead-mine."* Schoolcraft continues, *"In the interim, we went out to examine the lead-mine, which is situated in the west bank, and in the bottom of the river, as lumps of ore can be seen through the water, which is very clear and transparent. The ore is galena, or sulphuret of lead, accompanied by sulphuret of zinc, and imbedded in the bank of the river in a red clay."*[16]

Schoolcraft's work was widely read and may have stimulated interest in the James River area. There was already significant lead mining occurring in the eastern Ozarks and there would eventually be major lead discoveries in the western Ozarks near Joplin. Perhaps Galena adopted its name to attract potential mining interests. But it would be the water and not the mineral that would make Galena famous.

When Stone County was formed in 1851, the original county seat was established at Jamestown. This may have been the Jamestown that would eventually become Cape Fair or it may have been the initial name for the town of Galena. A deed recorded in 1856 says, "…which said Jamestown was subsequently changed to the name of Galena by an act of the General assembly of the State of Missouri approved January the thirteenth A.D. 1853."

As the county seat, Galena was the center of local government and grew as a commercial hub. On the tapered bench on the west shore of the river, a town square was platted. A log courthouse and log jail were built on the square. In 1855, a two story, wood frame courthouse was erected that would serve Stone County until 1920, when the present stone structure was built at the center of the square.

Galena grew slowly during the second half of the 19th century. As it did throughout all of Missouri, the Civil War and its aftermath of lawlessness had a chilling effect on the growth of Galena. The Ozarks was still an isolated area, difficult to get to and difficult to leave. But with the coming of the White River Railroad in 1904, Galena would be changed forever.

The people of the White River Valley knew the river. They knew its power and its secrets. The people of Galena plied the James like a highway. They floated timber down the swift course; they bathed and did laundry in the river; and they fished the waters.

The railroad brought outsiders to Galena who wanted to fish the streams and hunt the forested ridges. Many of the men who lived on the James willingly became river guides. In 1904 Charley, Herb and John Barnes started the Barnes Brothers Boating Company out of Galena. It was the first commercial float trip business in the area.[17] Many others joined the float fishing enterprise including Tom Yocum. Tom's family created a fishing camp on their farm along the James north of Galena. Camps were established all up and down the James to support float trips down to Branson and beyond.

Galena would become known as the "Float Capital of the World". The commerce created contributed significantly toward the prosperity of the Stone County seat.

The James River at Galena could only be crossed by ferry until a wagon bridge was built in 1915. This bridge coincided with the increasing popularity of automobile traffic. As roads in the area were slowly improved, the wagon bridge was replaced with the Y-bridge in 1927.

With the rest of the country, Galena suffered through the Depression years. In 1937, the last legal hanging in Missouri and perhaps the last public execution in the country was carried out on the town square. Roscoe "Red" Jackson was convicted of murdering traveling salesman Pearl Bozarth and was sentenced to die by the noose. The grisly event at a gallows constructed near the courthouse was viewed by hundreds and even filmed.

Dewey Jackson Short is perhaps Galena's best known citizen. He served twelve terms representing Missouri's 7th District in the United States Congress. Short supported development of the Table Rock project for many years and was known as a gifted orator. Dewey Short once said, "I know that without change there would be no progress, but I am not going to mistake mere change for progress."[18] The Dewey Short Visitor's Center at Table Rock Dam is named in his honor.

The building of Table Rock Lake brought an end to the great era of float fishing out of Galena. The town returned to a quieter time of handling county government business and supporting local agriculture and commerce. Local families remember the "river rats" who ran the James. Along the river, a few remnants of the fishing camps are visible. The James keeps flowing, sometimes low and slow and sometimes high and relentless.

Enon

Long Creek meanders up from the south. Yocum Creek flows in from the west. Just prior to converging, the two stream valleys form an anvil-shaped peninsula with a wide, gentle bench tapering down to the water. In this place of "much water", the little settlement of Enon, Arkansas grew up.

Goodspeed[19] writes of the area saying:

"John Yocum, from whom Yocum Creek derives its name, settled near Green Forest about 1833. He built a mill there at an early period in the history of the country."

Through the second half of the 19th century, the area around the confluence of Yocum and Long Creeks attracted trappers, homesteaders, timber cutters and occasional miners. The peaceful setting was isolated, but drew settlers who needed the services a small town could provide. By the early 20th century, the village provided a general store, post office, Baptist Church, a blacksmith and physician James Scott. The White River Division of the Missouri Pacific Railroad completed a line from Carthage, Missouri to Newport, Arkansas in 1906. The train ran through Omaha and Cricket, a few miles east of Enon, adding to the development of the area.

The Salem Baptist Church in nearby Denver may have established the satellite church at the little settlement around 1900. Anecdotal evidence attributes the name Enon Baptist Church to the scripture John 3:23 which references Salim, Aenon and water.

In 1901, an application was made to establish a post office for the area to be called Silver City. This name was rejected due to the postal service's reluctance to grant two-word names. The appellation "Enon" was substituted and accepted. William G. Hobbs was the first postmaster. It is believed the name Enon originated with the local church.

Despite never being incorporated or platted, Enon was important to those who lived nearby. Residents farmed the rough land, went to church and raised their families. But Enon remained isolated. The roads were very poor and with no bridge over Yocum or Long Creek, travel through the region was limited. There were fords over both creeks, but these were unreliable and often dangerous. Enon was just over the border from Boone County, far from the county seats of Harrison and Berryville. The Ozarks were still an isolated region and Enon was an isolated town. People produced most everything they needed on the farm. Emergencies were handled at home and disputes were settled without "outside" interference.

There were births and deaths, parties and feuds. Enon remained a viable town through the Depression and war years. By the 1950's, the "place of much water" had begun to decline. The local Underwood School was lost to consolidation in 1948. The last general store in town, owned by Fred Badley, burned in the early 50's. The post office was closed in 1955.

It's a long, lonely drive to the Enon Cemetery. Across Cricket Creek, up the ridge along a gradually deteriorating gravel drive. At the top, the forest thins to glades and reveals a natural vista out over Long Creek. The road slowly winds down into the valley and then deadends just above the creek. Here there are graves, depressions in the soil, rustic stone markers and substantial headstones. The site of Enon is just visible through the trees. It is a peaceful quiet setting.

Enon Store about 1905

The small towns and villages along the upper White River were the centers of life for the region. They provided supplies, services and a market for agricultural products. These towns were often the only link to the outside world for many residents. The post office was the primary source for communications and critical to the sustenance of any settlement.

Table Rock Lake changed all these towns. Some like Oasis were completely lost. Some like Radical were transformed into entirely new communities. Some like Golden and Viola retained just a name and a few memories. And some like Cape Fair and Shell Knob grew with the influx of people and development that the new lake brought.

Chapter 2
Archaeological Sites

The upper White River Valley was home to Native Americans for at least 10-12,000 years. During these millennia, the aboriginal peoples left many signs of their presence. Indian campsites were almost always near water. The alluvial terraces, bluff shelters and caves along the White River and its tributaries provided ideal locations for permanent and temporary habitation. These sites offered available water, proximity to food sources, and shelter or suitable settings for shelter for Native Americans. Many of these sites were buried by the waters of Table Rock Lake.

The earliest record of human habitation in the White River Valley consists of spear points dating to at least 10,000 BC. During the Paleo-Indian or Early Hunter period, indigenous peoples hunted mastodon, giant sloth, camel and large bison. These were a nomadic people who followed game trails and never stayed in one place for long. This period, at the end of the ice age, was characterized by cold weather, flooding exacerbated by melting glaciers and dust storms of fine loess. Water tables were much higher during the Early Hunter era. Temporary campsites were not necessarily on stream terraces. More likely, these early people made their homes on bluffs or ridges where flowing springs provided water. Paleo-Indian artifacts were found in the lower strata of the Rice and Jakie archaeological sites in Table Rock's lake bed.

American Indians became hunter/foragers during the Dalton period (8,000 BC-7,000 BC). These people primarily hunted, but with big game becoming extinct, they also did more gathering of edible plants. They also stayed in one location for longer periods. Cultural advances include the use of bone needles to fabricate fitted clothing, the use of nets for trapping small animals and fish, food processing tools, woodworking, and ceremonial practices. Evidence of Dalton habitation existed at the Rice, Jakie and Standlee I sites excavated during the construction of Table Rock.

The long Archaic period (7,000 BC to 1000 BC) saw the establishment of the Ozark Bluff Dwellers in the upper White River Valley. The Ozark Bluff Dwellers were unique to this area. Archaic peoples became less nomadic and often lived out of a semi-permanent home. Flint knapping became more specialized and produced implements like the Rice Lobed notched point and the Table Rock Stemmed dart point. Examples of Archaic ingenuity were excavated at Jakie Shelter off the Kings River: a ground stone celt for crushing food products and a full-grooved ax. Weaving plant fibers was practiced as well as some cultivation of plants. Ceremonial burials including the use of grave goods became a part of the lives of the Archaic peoples.

Several advances took place during the Woodland Period of 1000 BC-AD 900. Indians of the White River area began building houses, making pottery and growing crops. These technologies were probably imported from more advanced cultures like the Hopewell and Caddoan and adapted to the local environment. The spear and spear thrower were still the primary hunting weapons. Art objects, some crafted from exotic materials like mica, conch shell, obsidian and copper, were in use. Corn was cultivated for both consumption and ceremonial purposes.

Technological and socio-cultural advances continued into the Mississippian Period of AD 900-AD 1700. The Native Americans of this time developed a rich cultural life before the influence of European explorers. The people living in the area that would become Table Rock Lake were more isolated and the terrain was not amenable to large organized group living. Nevertheless, these people began using shell-tempered pottery, basketry, pipes and the bow and arrow. Farming became more widespread and involved plants other than maize. Evidence of these innovations was unearthed at the Jakie, Loftin and Lander I archaeological digs. The construction methods of Indian houses from this period can be ascertained from remains found at the Cantrell and Loftin sites. These Indian homes were built by placing vertical poles into the ground in a rectangular pattern. Smaller sticks and cane were woven into the uprights and then covered with a mixture of mud, grass and leaves. The roof was probably covered with thatch. Woven cane mats were likely used as floor and door coverings.

Ceremonial practices of the Mississippian era are indicated by burial practices, body adornment and mound building. The seventeen burials unearthed at Jakie Shelter yielded considerable information about the lives of these people. A ceremonial mound discovered at the Loftin site is one of very few known in the upper White River area. The building of a mound for cultural purposes was most likely an influence from more advanced Indian cultures, or it could possibly have been constructed by a visiting group. Whichever, the social development of the indigenous White River inhabitants had reached its culmination before the influence of other displaced Indian tribes and the encroachment of white settlers.

Starting with the explorations of De Soto in 1540, life began to change in the lodges and bluff dwellings along the White River and its tributaries. The introduction of trade goods is evidenced by finds at Indian shelters at the Jakie and Hardman sites. By the early 1700's, the Osage were hunting and living in southwestern Missouri. Over the next one hundred and fifty years, many different tribes would move through or temporarily live in the upper White River area including the Delaware, Shawnee, Kickapoo, Cherokee, Piankashaw, Peoria and Wea.

Some of the evidence of Indian life in this area is part of the historical record. The bulk of these peoples' lives is only told through the archaeological record. Fortunately, fairly extensive archaeological work was done by the Missouri Archaeological Society and others prior to the filling of Table Rock Lake. Unfortunately, almost all of these sites are now lost forever.[20]

Starting in the 1800's, the white settlers of this region began collecting Native American artifacts from the ancient shelters and campsites along the river bottomland. Many finds were made during cultivation of farm fields. Artifacts were generally viewed as curiosities. Many were retained by their finders in private collections. In 1922, Bushell, an archaeologist, described at least 20 sites he had located in the White and James River valleys, including one containing stone mortars and numerous shaped implements. In 1924, Harrington discovered and named the Ozark Bluff Dwellers from finds he made in the rock shelters along the upp ʃr White. From 1932 to 1942, Dellinger and Dickinson reported on additional studies they did on the Bluff Dwellers.[21] There was little other professional archaeological work done in the White River area prior to 1950.

The approval for the building of Table Rock Dam in 1941 and the expectation of its development in the late 40's were the impetus for considerable archaeological work done by the Missouri Archaeological Society under auspice of the University of Missouri. The University of Arkansas Museum in Fayetteville began archaeological surveys on sites in Arkansas in 1957.

In 1950, Lee Adams[22] surveyed sites within the White River watershed in Barry County. He located 120 surface sites and collected many stone artifacts. He performed excavations at four rock shelters, collecting numerous stone artifacts, pottery shards, woven baskets and skeletal remains. One of the shelters Adams studied was Hardman Cave near Shell Knob. Hardman Cave contained several projectile points, stone knives, scrapers, drills and antler handles. This site is now under the waters of Table Rock about one mile east of the Shell Knob Bridge on the south bank.

Lee Adams reported extensively on archaeological work in southwest Missouri in The Missouri Archaeologist in 1958.[23] This work examined hundreds of sites including many that would be inundated by Table Rock. The sites had been identified over a 30 year period.

Adams researched a large site on the Stubblefield farm about three miles above the Eagle Rock Bridge. This was also the site of the Calloway Ford. Stone points, a mortar and several pottery shards were collected here. The pottery was of a worked, decorated, stone-tempered type. Several smaller sites along the White between the Stubblefield farm and Roaring River yielded a variety of Native American relics.

A significant archaeological site was researched at the Easley homestead at the mouth of Roaring River. Like many sites in the study, the area was an active farm. The location included cultivated land on the narrow bottoms, the Easley home and outbuildings, stone walls and a spring. Numerous stone implements representing various cultural periods were found at Easley. In addition, many pioneer relics were unearthed in the area including wagon parts and camping equipment.

The Easley ford and ferry crossed the White at this location. On the east side of the mouth of Roaring River, an ancient stone grave was discovered. It contained bone fragments from two adult humans and dogs.

Adams examined several small sites along the entire length of Roaring River. In addition to many stone implements from various cultural periods, several disturbed stone cairns or burial structures were found. The Roaring River valley archaeological research indicated it was a popular Indian campsite location for a long period of time.

Indian campsites were noted all along the upper White. At the mouth of Rock Creek at Devil's Backbone, a large site was examined. Many artifacts including projectile points, flint axes and tools made of sandstone, flint and quartzite were found at this location.

Adams' survey revealed Indian artifacts at several sites around the confluence of the White, Kings and Mill Creek. A small cave just south of the mouth of Mill Creek was reported to contain charcoal, fragments of mussel shell, flint chips and broken arrowheads.

In his 1958 report, Adams identified numerous sites along the James and Kings Rivers and in the Baxter Indian Creek area. Some of the larger, more important sites are discussed elsewhere in this chapter. Many of the smaller finds were not researched further due to the impending development of the Table Rock Project.

Adams' extensive research reveals that the entire White River watershed was home to Native Americans over a very long time period. Evidence of habitation exists from the Paleo-Indian period 10,000 years ago up to the historic era when the Osage began to interact with white settlers. The ubiquity of stone implements, points and other artifacts found near almost every stream of any consequence indicates how attractive the White River Valley was to these early inhabitants.

Starting in 1951, Carl H. Chapman, renowned Missouri archaeologist, helped organize the Table Rock Salvage Project.[24] This large-scale undertaking coordinated by the University of Missouri and the Missouri Archaeological Society did an excellent job of researching the entire Table Rock basin in Missouri with limited funding and time. Over 800 sites were identified and several were excavated, yielding considerable invaluable information about the culture and time frame of the Native American inhabitants of the White River basin. Without this work, this knowledge would have been lost forever beneath Table Rock.

Chapman and his associates faced a daunting challenge. The area to be surveyed and studied was very large and contained many sites. The terrain was very rugged and roads were generally poor if existing at all. Many of the bottomland sites had been under cultivation for years. This accounted for large numbers of items removed by area farmers. Other potential sites were in pasture making it difficult to locate surface artifacts. The local populace was very helpful in allowing access to their property, helping locate sites and sharing their previous finds. Chapman developed methods to improve the efficiency of his task, including search teams, trenching and the use of grid pattern excavation.

A typical search team consisted of four persons who would hire a floatboat, put in at a location several miles upstream and float back down the river. One or two members of the team would disembark to do a ground search of terraces, hillslopes and small tributary streams. The others would stay in the boat and scan the bluffs with binoculars looking for caves, rock shelters or other likely sites. Potential sites were given a cursory examination and recorded on a map for later, more thorough investigation. Search teams could cover about a mile of river valley in a day. This method yielded hundreds of sites.

Starting in 1955, on major open sites, a trench digger was employed to allow quick identification of the various strata of specimens. Where feasible, the Table Rock Salvage Project used grid pattern excavation to assist in classifying and aging artifacts. Marking the area off in grid squares allowed a more careful identification of the items located.[25]

Two campsites were documented on Long Creek. The Pinkley site near the intersection of Jakes Branch and Long Creek contained many shaped stone artifacts. At the McFarland site, located one mile above the White, an ancient hearth was uncovered. Robber Cave and Hellgrammite Shelter in the bluffs above Long Creek were searched and found to contain a few artifacts from the Mississippian period.

There were several campsites discovered on the large river terraces along the White just above the dam site. The Vaughn, Lewellyn and Haggard sites were spread out across the west bank. Initially, only a few artifacts were recovered from these sites, but local residents reported previously collecting many items including a human skull from this area. In 1955, archaeological work was performed at the Vaughn sites during basin excavation for Table Rock Lake. Several relics were collected scattered throughout the site and evidence was found of five human burials. Similar collection took place during this time at the Lewellyn site yielding several worked stone pieces and one burial site.

Four miles up the White, the Cantrell sites yielded an important find. Using the trench digger, the remains of an Indian house were uncovered. This dig presented useful information about the home building and life style of the Mississippian peoples. Some artifacts and pottery shards from these sites were from the earlier Woodland period (500 BC- 400 AD).

Several campsites and rock shelters were studied by the Table Rock Salvage Project in the Cow Creek area. These sites lay on the south bank of the White on terraces on both sides of Cow Creek. One site just below Little Cow Creek was known locally as the Indian Cemetery. Although no human remains were located during the survey, many stone artifacts were found over a large area. Some evidence of occupation was obtained from two rock shelters, one at the head of Little Cow Creek and the other at the probable source of Little Cow's main tributary.

Just above the old Kimberling Bridge, a river terrace on the south side yielded many stone implements. Two campsites on the north side had previously revealed tools and a pottery shard. Perhaps one of the most promising areas surveyed during the Table Rock Salvage Project was where the James meets the White. Several sites on the terraces northwest of the confluence were studied including Loftin and Philibert. The initial surface investigation of these sites in 1951 produced only limited artifacts, probably due to frequent flooding. In 1956, more extensive testing was performed revealing evidence of a possible ceremonial mound at the Loftin site.

The remains of at least five Indian dwellings were unearthed at Loftin. These structures had designs similar to Caddoan and early Mississippian cultures. These similarities indicate influence or trade between the White River inhabitants and the more advanced Caddoan peoples around 1000-1200 AD. The Caddoan Indian culture, centered around the Arkansas River basin, had developed engraved pottery, specialized socio-religious practices and some forms of maize cultivation. The peoples who inhabited the Loftin site most likely had contact with or were influenced by the Caddoan culture.[26]

Along with the Philibert site, this area was giving up information that it had once been an important location for Mississippian and possibly earlier peoples. There was also material uncovered indicating the presence of the homestead and possible trading post established here in 1833 by Joseph Philibert. Unfortunately, bad weather and flood conditions in early 1957 and 1958 severely restricted additional archaeological work at these and most other sites in the Table Rock basin.

The Salvage Project did not do extensive surveying along the James watershed. Surface examinations at a campsite and rock shelter just north of Aunts Creek's confluence with the James yielded some stone artifacts and shell-tempered pottery fragments. In 1956, further work at Aunts Creek Shelter produced numerous tools, pottery shards, a fishhook, and bone and antler implements. Several interesting artifacts were found in Magers Cave on the James. The dig team collected several pottery shards which they were able to reconstruct into a vessel. The pot was a shaped, shell-tempered and fired vessel. It was one of the few reconstructed pottery pieces found in the Table Rock area. Magers Cave also contained a hearth with evidence of turtle, turkey and deer bones.

Many campsites and rock shelters were studied in the Little and Big Indian Creek area. Four small sites on the upper end of Big Indian near Book Hollow and one near the old 86 bridge contained a few traces of implements. A campsite was documented on the west shore of the White River opposite the mouth of Big Indian.

Several bluff shelters were surveyed along Little Indian Creek. A cluster of shelters located near the headwaters contained little evidence of habitation. A large shelter south of Lampe containing stone artifacts and two pottery shards was not within the Table Rock Lake boundaries.

A campsite at Look Out Point near Baxter was reported to yield several shaped stone pieces. Nearby, the Indian Creek Shelter was classified as a true Ozark Bluff Dwelling. Due to its dry condition, the remains of several perishable items gave some insight into the Bluff Dwellers' culture. Basket-lined pits were unearthed containing agricultural products including corn, pumpkin or squash, gourd and sunflowers. Evidence of gathered foods included chinquapin nuts, burr oak acorns, hickory nuts, black walnuts, hazel nuts, hackberry, pawpaw, persimmon, wild rye, wild plum and grape seeds. Basketry items and rabbit fur string were also found. This interesting discovery could not be attributed to a particular time period during the Table Rock Salvage Project.[27]

The Lander Shelter I located near present day Big Indian Park revealed evidence of occupation over a long period of time. Shaped stone artifacts and pottery remains indicated use of this site during the Archaic (7000-1000 BC), Middle Woodland (500 BC-400 AD) and Mississippian (900-1700 AD) periods. Skeletal burial remains were also associated with this dig. The two Andoc Shelters on the north bank of Horseshoe Bend contained fairly recent Indian implements.

About 1½ miles below Big Indian Creek on the White's eastern bluff was Porter Shelter. This site contained evidence of hearths, storage pits and several interesting pottery and stone vessels.

One of the most important sites investigated as part of the Table Rock Salvage Project was the Rice Site. This site, named for the property owner D.H. Rice (sites were often named for the existing land owner), was located on the west side of Mill Creek about a quarter mile above its confluence with the White, just southwest of Campbell Point. Archaeological work was performed at this bluff shelter in 1952 and 1953 under the direction of Carl Chapman.

The Rice Site was an attractive shelter for Native Americans. It had a fairly large (about 400 square feet) covered area and faced southeast, providing warmth from the sun and protection from north winds. There was a nearby spring, but the shelter itself remained dry.

Edible foods which could be gathered in the area included black walnut, chestnut, acorns, hackberry, may apple, pawpaw, butternut, hazelnut, gooseberry, serviceberry, strawberry, wild plum, persimmon, frost grape, black haw, ragweed, muscadine and sumpweed. Animals available to these early hunters were deer, elk, bear, possibly bison, panther, bobcat, wolf, beaver, otter, muskrat, mink, raccoon, skunk, possum, rabbit, squirrel, fox, quail, passenger pigeon and turkey. The streams contained eel, gar, turtles, crappie, sucker, sunfish, catfish, walleye, bass and edible mussels. Remains of some of these food sources were identified at the Rice site. Based on bone fragments, deer was the most popular meat eaten by these early inhabitants.

Based on the type and style of artifacts excavated at Rice, three distinct cultural complexes were found to have inhabited the shelter- an Early, Middle and Late. These complexes correspond to the Archaic through Mississippian Periods.

Many shaped tools were unearthed at the Rice site including projectile points, scrapers, knives, manos, grinding stones and drills. One specific shaped projectile point found in the area was named the Rice Lobed. Other relics included shaped antlers, shell beads, stone pipes and bone punches. Pottery shards were discovered, particularly in the upper levels of the dig. Evidence of pottery, some decorated, included sand-, grit- and shell-tempered forms.

The excavation at the Rice Site uncovered seven human burials. The graves revealed a variety of remains from just a few fragments to an almost complete skeleton. Two of the graves included stones placed over the body. Some of the burials appeared to include offerings such as projectile points and a stone axe. One interment included the bones of a dog.

The Rice Site is important because of the number and quality of artifacts recovered from a long continuum of human habitation. This site revealed the historical importance of the archaeological work done in the area that would soon be forever covered by the deep water of Table Rock Lake.[28]

In 1956, Carl H. Chapman reported on studies done on several sites in Barry County.[29] Pettigrew Cave on the Kings River about ½ mile above the present-day Hwy. 86 bridge contained items like arrowheads and pottery. Hardman Cave was found to contain artifacts from three different cultural periods suggesting use over a long period of time. Across the river from Hardman, Kimball Shelter yielded several shaped flint implements, shell-tempered pottery shards and skeletal burial remains including grave goods.

From 1955 through 1956, the Table Rock Salvage Project excavated some very important sites on the upper Kings River-Jakie Shelter, the Standlee sites and the Crisp Shelters. Jakie was a large rock shelter about a half mile up Jakie Hollow from the Kings. The Standlee and Crisp sites were in the Big Hollow valley area south of Jakie.

Excavation at Jakie Shelter revealed evidence of use over a prolonged period of time. A variety of artifacts were found in the different layers excavated. Seventeen burial sites were found at Jakie. One of the skeletons was deemed to be that of a "medicine woman". Along with her remains was an interesting assortment of personal belongings including beads, awls, a whistle, red ocher and a flint knife. The other skeletal finds ranged from the remains of infants to adults. It was hoped the bones would yield information on the life style and diseases of these early people. The Jakie Stemmed point is named for the unique shaped stone blades found at this site. They date from 5000-4000 BC.

An "open house" was held at the Jakie site in May, 1956. Over 5000 people from the area visited the dig site to view the archaeological work in progress.

Keith Shumaker of Golden, Mo. worked at the Jakie Shelter site in 1956. Keith was one of three local young men hired by the Table Rock Salvage Project to assist with the dig at Jakie. Local help was employed to help locate possible archaeological sites and also to work the digs. Keith was paid $1.25 an hour for his hard work at Jakie.

Carl Chapman and Robert Bray of the University of Missouri and other members of the Missouri Archaeological Society oversaw the work at Jakie Shelter. Keith Shumaker described the site as a large bluff shelter with a significant overhang in the bluff wall next to Jakie Creek. The shelter was "dry" in that it did not have water flowing through it and was protected from the elements. Archaeological relics are typically much better preserved in a "dry" shelter. The area in and around the bluff shelter was marked off in a grid pattern with each square given its own identification. Using a mattock, Keith and the others working the site scraped away the soil looking for ashes, flint chips or any other sign of human habitation. If an interesting stratum was found, a small shovel, trowel and paint brush were used to carefully outline and remove an object. Bones were of particular interest.

Keith Shumaker was digging in one of the grid squares when his mattock struck something unusual. He immediately informed Bob Bray and upon further examination, they uncovered a human skull. This find was the burial of the "medicine woman" found at Jakie.

Keith remembers the open house held at Jakie Shelter as being a very large event with thousands of visitors coming from the region to view the archaeological work. To accommodate the big crowd, the road to Jakie was improved by grading. Local Boy Scouts, Sheriff's deputies and several members of the Missouri Archaeological Society were recruited for crowd control and as guides.

Keith says the local store ran out of refreshments well before noon. Shumaker says he learned a lot from Chapman and Bray and is glad he had the experience working at Jakie Shelter.

The "medicine woman" burial at Jakie Shelter

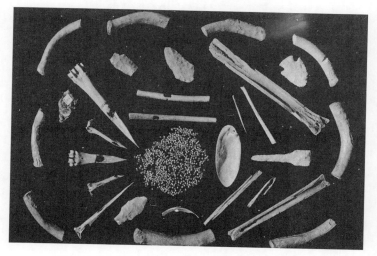
"Medicine woman" artifacts from Jakie Shelter

Open house at Jakie Shelter

Robert Bray at Jakie Shelter

The study done at the Standlee shelters, particularly Standlee I in Big Hollow also yielded useful scientific information. Standlee I was a fairly shallow opening, but a considerable number of ancient artifacts were found in the midden in front of the rock shelter, including a Dalton Serrated stone point dating the site to about 8000BC. The site showed little or no evidence of more recent Indian occupation.

Crisp Shelter I and II in Big Hollow produced several items including stone and pottery smoking pipes, grit-tempered pottery, a mussel shell pendant and stone and shell beads. Crisp Shelter III on the Kings River contained many artifacts including modern debris. The site had been previously disturbed making it impossible to classify items by strata.

The Epperly Cave was located on the White River opposite the mouth of the Kings River at the top of a steep slope. Pottery shards, projectile points and stone implements were unearthed at this site. The Epperly Cairn on the hill above Epperly Cave appeared to be a stone burial structure. It had been previously disturbed and only a few human bone fragments were found.

The Table Rock Salvage Project gives us a glimpse into the lives of the original human inhabitants of the upper White River Valley. Like the white settlers who followed them, they were a rugged people living off the land. They sustained themselves on what the land provided. The bluffs and terraces afforded shelter. The forests and streams gave them food and materials. There are even indications that these people had a spiritual life. Burials with grave goods indicate at least a respect for life and a possible belief in a higher spiritual power.

These archaeological sites are almost all covered by the lake now. They will reveal no more secrets about life in this valley before the historical era. We owe a gift of thanks to the hard working members of the Table Rock Salvage Project and the other archaeologists who toiled under difficult conditions to extract as much information as possible from the sites that would be buried under Table Rock Lake.

Chapter 3
Farms, Homesteads and Cemeteries

Construction of Table Rock Dam was authorized by the United States Congress through the Flood Control Act of 1941 for "flood control and hydroelectric power, and other beneficial water uses". World War II, the Korean Conflict and the Corps' decision to build Bull Shoals first, delayed the building of Table Rock for several years. Construction of the project was awarded to Morrison-Knudsen Company, Inc. and Utah Construction Company.

Table Rock's lake bed consisted of large forested areas and rich river bottomland prior to the dam's construction. The area to be inundated was typical Ozark highland forest of primarily mixed hardwood and cedar trees. The White River bottomland contained many small farms and homesteads. The United States government purchased all private land within the project's boundaries.

Land purchases began in the early 50's and were finalized in 1961. Just over 43,000 acres up to the planned conservation pool elevation of 915 feet above sea level comprised most of the lake basin. Acreage between 915' and 931', the flood control pool level, required the acquisition of 9200 acres. An additional 5,501 acres above 931' comprised flowage easement rights. Flowage easement parcels, which may be periodically flooded by Table Rock, can be privately owned, but not developed. The total project acreage, excluding easements, was 57,806.

The purchase of private land caused considerable consternation among many inhabitants of the White River Valley. Many families had lived on family farms for generations. Many would lose their homes. Some residents welcomed the opportunity to sell.

In 1955, the Corps of Engineers opened a real estate office in Branson to acquire project land. They also published a booklet and held public meetings explaining their purchase policies. Nevertheless, there was much confusion on the issues. There was particular misunderstanding about the obtaining of property between 923 and 936 feet elevations. These acquisitions involved a complicated formula involving flowage easements, topography and land contour changes.

Property values were determined by appraisers who inspected the property, interviewed owners and performed "comparables" to other similar, recently sold tracts. From the appraisal, all land owners were presented with an "Option for Purchase of Land" indicating the price the government would pay for the property. Owners were usually paid for their land within 90 days of signing an option.

If the owner refused the offered price, a condemnation proceeding was begun. Under these circumstances, the government was forced to condemn the land and take ownership under eminent domain. This procedure entailed a court proceeding before the U.S. District Court in which the land owner could present three alternate appraisals. Typically, the owner made a case to receive the highest of these appraisals. Condemnation proceedings were also used in cases where defective land titles existed. In 1958, the appraisal process was changed to require at least two appraisals- one from a Corps staff member and one from a professional contract appraiser. Land owners could receive partial payment, up to the government's appraisal amount, before resolution of condemnation proceedings.

Improvements to property could be removed at the owner's expense. The value of improvements removed was deducted from the amount paid for the land. Owners could also be reimbursed for crops which could not be harvested. Timber in sufficient quantity and quality to be considered merchantable could also be sold to the government. The land owner had the option to remove any timber themselves prior to acceptance of an option to buy.

Owners and tenants of property within the Table Rock Project could request reimbursement of moving expenses not to exceed 25% of the parcel value. Land owners were allowed to remain on their property until the project required them to leave. Those who accepted the government's offer could stay for a specified period. Those who forced condemnation proceedings could remain on their land under a lease. Most were allowed to stay on their property until October 1956. Some who refused to sell were ordered off by April 1956. This apparent discrimination was opposed and ultimately the Corps changed this policy. At the time of the June 1957 flood when Table Rock filled almost to a 900 foot level, many farms were still growing crops in the bottomland. The flood wiped out all the unharvested crops. Property owners who lost assets in the flood were entitled to some form of recompense from the Federal government.

About 4600 acres of Mark Twain National Forest were transferred to the Corps of Engineers. 3294 acres of this land was a large tract in the Cow Creek area. The remaining acreage ceded consisted of many small parcels within the lake's boundaries up to the 936 feet flowage easement.

While work on Table Rock Dam began in 1954 and progressed swiftly, completion of much of the work in the lake bed was delayed. Much of the delay was caused by the postponement of funding approval through Congress. As late as February 1958, bids were still being let on land clearing contracts. Cemetery relocation was not started until 1957, much of it after a spring flood of that year filled the entire lake bed. Some cemeteries on the upper ends of the lake were not relocated until late 1958. Land acquisition had also proceeded slowly. In early 1958, many land parcels had not yet been appraised. Some local residents who had reached agreement on selling their property had not been paid.

Delays also occurred on the construction of bridges and the re-routing of roads. The initial delays were caused when the project managers, the states and the local counties could not agree on the replacement projects. The floods of 1957 and 1958 exacerbated these delays. The lack of useable roads and bridges during the floods caused considerable inconvenience for local people.

By the end of 1958, most of these problems had been resolved.

All of the major road building was complete or nearly complete. All the major bridges were in use except the Central Crossing span at Shell Knob, which was opened for use in 1959.

Despite these concerns, once the dam conduits were closed in December 1958, the lake began to fill for the last time.

Precipitation fell on the watershed and inexorably water flowed from the springs, the creeks and the streams. It poured down the White, James and Kings Rivers and piled up behind Table Rock Dam. Everything in the lake bed was flooded forever.

The people of the White River valley were hardy and independent. They valued the land, family, hard work and education. Living in the Ozarks had never been easy. Those who lost their homes to Table Rock Lake had often struggled to make a living here. After the big lake came, some left the area, but many stayed to continue farming or to operate businesses. Some took advantage of the new economic resource created by Table Rock.

The following stories are based on actual interviews with people who lived on farms and homes that were lost to Table Rock Lake.

Bob Philibert

Bob Philibert's great-grandfather, Joseph Philibert, came to the James River area in 1822 to help establish a trading post with William Gillis at Delaware Town, four and one half miles west of what is today Nixa. Joseph first worked as a gunsmith and then as a clerk at the trading post.

Delaware Town was an extended village inhabited by Delaware Indians, a semi-nomadic tribe. The Delaware lived in several villages along the James growing crops and trading furs. The Delaware were relocated in 1830 to the Kansas City area with Gillis' oversight.

Gillis' trading post at Delaware Town consisted of several log buildings including a two-room house, a retail store, a warehouse and several outbuildings. Joseph Philibert made trips to St. Genevieve occasionally to obtain supplies and goods for the post. The 250 mile trip took at least fifteen days of travel by wagon along the Old Piney Creek Road.

After traveling to several locations throughout the Midwest while working for Gillis, Philibert returned to Stone County in 1833. He married 16 year-old Peninah Yoachum of the legendary "silver dollar" Yoachums. Philibert homesteaded property along the ridge north of the confluence of the James and White Rivers. He farmed the land and possibly operated a trading post here until his death in 1884. Philibert Bluff above the old homestead bears the name of the original white resident.

In the 1950's, Bob Philibert owned 40 acres on the south bank of the White River about three miles east of Shell Knob. He was offered $20 an acre for 20 acres of the property during construction of the Table Rock Project. Bob refused the offer and forced a condemnation proceeding. He still received $20 an acre. In 1957, Mr. Philibert had cut and stacked a quantity of oak staves on his remaining property. The staves were all washed away in the flood of that year. Bob and Willena Philibert resided in their home on their remaining property next to the lake for many years.

Jewel R. (Hutchens) Farwell

Jewel Hutchens was born in 1921 on the Wire Road in Barry County. She was educated at Missouri State Teachers College (now Missouri State University) and Drury. As a girl, she visited Pineville to see the production of the 1939 movie "Jesse James". Her father supplied two horses for the movie and her brother was an extra. She met the actors Jane Darwell, Henry Fonda and Tyrone Power.

Jewel also remembers visiting the White River to camp at Eagle Rock and Easley Ford. A ferry boat had broken loose up river at Lewis Ford and wrecked at Easley Ford. The vessel was partially buried in the river bed and provided a swim platform for Jewel and her companions.

She moved to the Eagle Rock area in 1944 to teach school. Jewel married Ray Farwell in 1945 and lived until just recently within view of the Eagle Rock Bridge over Table Rock Lake.

Jewel and Ray Farwell at the Farwell Bridge 1945

Ray Farwell's great-grandfather Albert Farwell bought several hundred acres on either side of the White River in 1858. He farmed the bottomland on both sides of the present site of the Eagle Rock Bridge. Albert grew corn and wheat and had an orchard.

Jewel Farwell relates the following about Albert Farwell:

"Ray's great-grandfather Albert went to take some supplies to Pea Ridge. They were having a battle there in 1862 in March. It was raining and he caught a bad cold. It went into pneumonia and he died. He only lived here not very long. He left five or six children and his widow.

So one night the bushwackers came. She (Albert's widow) heard them out there. They were trying to get her cattle and horses. She was fighting them. They went clear off down to the river bank. They hit her in the head and she was laying down there. She finally came to and got back to the house.

When she did, the oldest daughter said, 'Well, we got to leave here. We don't have protection. No men with us.' What they did was mortgage the farm and got enough money to move into Cassville until the war was over.

This oldest daughter was a teacher. She started teaching when she was seventeen. She was the first woman from Barry County to graduate from the University of Missouri. She only lived to 27 years old. She had typhoid. She never married. She felt like she was the one supposed to take care of the family. She taught long enough to pay off that mortgage."

The Farwells managed to keep most of their land in the family to the present. When Jewel moved to the farm in 1945, the home was located on the east side of the river. There was an older three room house on the property below the bridge crossing the White. This building was used as a construction office during erection of the Farwell Bridge in the late 30's. There was a hand-dug well at this site. Remnants of this well can still be seen below the Eagle Rock swimming beach at low water levels. The Farwell cemetery is still located within the Eagle Rock campground. At least two graves were moved from the bottomland to the existing cemetery during development of Table Rock.

Ray and Jewel farmed and ran cattle along the White River. Early on, there was no electricity at the farm. They drew water by hand from the old well. The Farwells used a gas refrigerator. Jewel liked to read books by the light of an Aladdin lamp. She enjoyed reading books like *Gone with the Wind* to Ray. Ray hunted and fished the river.

Route P, a gravel road, came up from the Arkansas line, crossed the White and traveled on to Eagle Rock and Cassville. This was a farm-to-market route serving area farms and providing access to the railheads. Local ranchers like Ray Farwell would drive herds of cattle and pigs to Cassville, Exeter or Eureka Springs. The cattle trail followed old Route F along Roaring River, a rough road crossing the stream several times.

In the mid-1950's, the Farwells were offered $139 an acre for their river bottomland along the White. Portions of their property would become Highway 86, approaches to the new Eagle Rock Bridge, the Eagle Rock Corps Park and Marina and Table Rock Lake.

Ray Farwell was not happy about losing portions of his land. He knew he would miss the river. Jewel relates, "My husband didn't like the lake. He didn't like to fish in it. He loved to fish in that river. He'd get the best fish out of there- channel cat. Have you ever eaten channel cat? It's very good. Sometimes he had what he called a trot line and limb lines. You had to get up early because a lot of times they'd break loose. Good for breakfast."

When the White flooded in 1957, the Eagle Rock Bridge was covered with water. Ray ferried people across the deluge in his aluminum boat. After Table Rock was completed, Ray and Jewel continued to farm and ranch their remaining land. Ray eventually started an excavation business, taking advantage of the building boom occurring around the new reservoir. They also built and operated the Farwell Court lake resort. The Farwells raised their family along the White River and then Table Rock Lake. Their descendants continue to live and work in the Eagle Rock area- a landscape altered, but still retaining some of the qualities that attracted Albert Farwell 150 years ago.

Phyllis (Carney) Owens

Phyllis Carney was born in 1942 in a two-story wood frame house on the banks of James River. The Carney homestead was on the high terrace on the north side of Wilson Ford about ½ mile east of Piney Creek. Phyllis' grandfather, Charlie Carney, was a schoolteacher and farmed the land along the James. Phyllis' father, Orie Carney, was born on the farm and ran a Hereford cattle operation there until eminent domain took most of his property in 1956.

Phyllis lived at the isolated farmstead during her childhood with her parents Orie and Blanche Carney, her sister Claudene and their hired hand Bill Costlow. Most people would have thought it a wild and lonely place, but Phyllis loved it. On hot days, she could swim in the river shoals with her dog Rex at Wilson Ford or Cole Ford. Cole Ford was about a mile upriver adjoining property the Carneys owned around Buzzard Hollow. Phyllis also spent a lot of time riding her horse.

Phyllis Carney and Rex at Cole Ford

Phyllis' grandmother, Alice Clark, lived on the other side of Wilson Ford. Phyllis and her parents would paddle across the river in an old boat to visit her grandmother. Orie would haul a bucket of sand from the river up to the porch for Phyllis to play in. She had a wind-up toy bulldozer that she retained as a prized possession for many years.

During harvest, Phyllis helped her daddy with farm chores. At seven she was driving the hay truck and at nine, she drove the tractor hauling hay and oats across the steep pasture hillsides. On cold mornings, Phyllis helped milk cows. Her mother strained the milk through cheesecloth and churned some into butter. Phyllis drank the milk warm.

The Carneys raised cattle, hogs, goats and sheep. They grew hay, corn and oats for livestock feed and tended a vegetable garden. They kept horses for riding and farm work. Each year, Phyllis would raise a kid or lamb. The sheep were sheared for wool until the losses from coyotes became too limiting.

Blanche Carney tended a chicken operation. She would purchase live chicks and raise them for meat and eggs. Phyllis relates her mother's determination toward her chickens in the following story:

> *"Them chickens was my mama's and they were a serious business. I remember one time daddy's old sow got to killin' 'em. He was at the barn and she heard the chickens squawking. She went out the door and she hollored, 'Orie, you better get your old sow, I'm gonna kill her!' And she would of. Didn't take daddy long to get his old sow out of the chickens."*

The Carney barn

The Carney homestead consisted of an old unpainted wood frame house, a large, sturdy barn and several outbuildings. There was no electricity until 1954. Their light came from kerosene lamps. The only running water was from a windmill supplying a large cattle trough. Later, Orie Carney ran a water line from the windmill to the back porch and eventually piped the water into the kitchen. Water was heated on the wood stove. They owned a battery operated radio. Phyllis remembers listening to the news, the Lone Ranger and the Grand Ole Opry. The highlight of the year was a trip to Springfield's Ozark Empire Fair.

The road leading to and from the Carney place was very rugged. It ran along the James' north terrace and then followed Piney Creek for about one mile before heading north to cross Woolly Creek. The old road stayed north until intersecting State Highway C about three miles west of Cape Fair. Parts of this road were gravel, but some sections were nothing more than trails cleared down to ledgerock. It was three miles and thirty minutes from the Carney's home to their mailbox. The road was not a county road and part of it ran through National Forest. Orie did what he could to maintain this link to the outside world. He dragged a horse-drawn road grader across the rough spots, but it didn't help much. A tire patch kit and a hand pump were necessities as the old '36 Ford pickup often experienced flat tires. Phyllis says about the road: "If I see someone down there that I knew when I was a little kid, the first thing they'll say is, 'I remember how rough that road was getting down to your house.' I think they remember that more than they remember me." If it snowed, the road was basically impassable. Blanche Carney always made sure to stock up supplies for the winter. An alternate route from the Carney homestead ran north crossing Cole Ford before connecting with Route Y. The road crossed Bear Den Hollow and hugged the shore of the James before reaching the old Cape Fair Bridge. This route was useful only when the river was low enough to cross at Cole Ford.

Orie Carney liked to gig for suckers in the James. In the fall he and his hired hand Bill would take out the old wooden rowboat they kept at Cole Ford. Fishing the river, often at night, they gigged fish with a long-handled gigging pole. The scaled, filleted and scored suckers made a hearty meal. Blanche Carney would usually can some of the fillets.

The early 1950's were drought years. Piney Creek all but dried up, but the James still ran cool and clear. The Carney's cattle were pastured on the other side of Cole Ford along Route Y. To provide water for their livestock, they had to haul water. Orie bought a couple of large galvanized tanks of about 250 gallons each and placed them in the pasture. He borrowed a 500 gallon stock tank from a neighbor. The tank was loaded onto the hay trailer and hauled to Cole Ford. Orie, Bill and Phyllis filled the tank by hand with river water and carted it to their thirsty cattle.

By 1956, the Carneys knew there was plenty of water coming. Table Rock Dam was under construction on the mighty White. All but 19 acres of their property were sold through eminent domain to the U.S. Government. The barn was dismantled and partially rebuilt at a new site near Cape Fair. Some lumber was salvaged from the old house, but the rest of the homestead was bulldozed down to the foundations.

Phyllis (Carney) Owens says she is still bitter about the loss of her home. She admits it may have been beneficial for her parents. It was getting more difficult to make the farm productive due to their isolated location. The Carneys moved to Cape Fair in 1956 and ran a Holstein dairy operation- but it wasn't the same as it had been on the river. Phyllis married Glen Owens whose father was born in the Owens Bend area and seldom returns to the area of her childhood. Phyllis reminisces:

"I liked it down there. I was perfectly happy right there. I liked the cows and was always outside with daddy. That was a sad day when the cows left. He kept twelve of them when we moved to Cape Fair in 1956, but sold them a couple years later."

Phyllis Carney lived her idyllic childhood on the banks of the James River. Her home sat between elevation 900 and 915 feet. Now when Table Rock Lake is low, you can see the remnants of the barn, the house and the windmill. Perhaps as the wind whispers across the lake's surface, you can discern the giggles of a happy little girl, splashing with her dog at the ford.

Scotty Chamberlin

Scotty Chamberlin was born in Springfield, Mo. in 1935. At six weeks of age, he and his mother were paddled across the James River to Camp Rock Haven. This would be his home off and on for the next several years.

Scotty's parents Lyle and Alma (Pat) Chamberlain (different spellings were used) purchased the Aurora Fishing Clubhouse in 1930. The Clubhouse was located on the west bank of the James River across from Bear Den Hollow south of Cape Fair. The Aurora Clubhouse was used by area sportsmen interested in hunting and fishing. The building was constructed around the turn of the century with lumber hauled from Aurora by horse and wagon.

Aurora Clubhouse

Lyle Chamberlain was looking for an opportunity to earn a living in the difficult times of the Depression. He liked to fish and take photographs and planned to develop a fishing resort on the river.

The Chamberlains built several cabins and established Camp Rock Haven. They generally kept about thirteen johnboats and catered to clients interested in float fishing. The original johnboats were wooden craft purchased locally. Later, Camp Rock Haven had Aurora Metal Works copy the wooden boats in aluminum. In 1934, the Aurora Clubhouse burned down and the Chamberlains built a new home on the remaining foundation.

Scotty Chamberlin lived and worked on the river for much of his younger life. As a boy he didn't guide much, but was responsible for much of the equipment associated with the float service. He organized all the gear necessary for a day's float. The commissary included boats, chairs and paddles, food, ice chests, cooking utensils, tents, cots and bedding. Scotty helped gather the gear, load the johnboats and transport the float clients to their put-in site. As a youth, Scotty would shuttle anglers to and from the river in a 1 ½ ton Chevy long-bed truck. The vehicle was a converted Coca-Cola truck with dual rear tires. Scotty learned early to navigate the rough river roads. The roads were not much more than trails, cleared down to ledgerock and graveled, often just one lane. Punctures were frequent on the flint strewn roads and Scotty became efficient at repairing flats on the rayon tires.

Scotty Chamberlin's first guide job

In the evening, many float anglers would return from the river to Camp Rock Haven. They would eat supper at the Rock Haven Cafe (later the Fisherman's Hat Cafe) operated by Alma Chamberlain with the assistance of some of the float guides' wives. During the winter, the Chamberlains would hold lively square dances at the camp.

Scotty's work continued with cleaning, sorting and restocking the equipment for the next day's float. Laundry at the camp was cleaned in an old wringer washer, hung out to dry and pressed in an "Ironrite". For several years, the only electricity at Camp Rock Haven was supplied by a Delco gasoline-powered generator. The generator charged a bank of batteries which powered lights, refrigerators, pumps and equipment. Ozark Electric ran power to the area after World War II. The original well at Camp Rock Haven was a hand-dug well. Later, a mechanically drilled well was bored on the property. Rock Haven was the first location to have telephone service on the lower James. Lyle Chamberlain had an early mobile phone in his 1932 Ford. The wireless system connected to Marionville and then Springfield. The telephone number was ZF 8 2256.

Camp Rock Haven was located on the river bottomland near the end of the original Cape Fair Bridge. The river often flooded, not only covering the bridge, but causing damage to the camp. After a flood, the Chamberlains had to thoroughly clean and repair the cabins. On one occasion, the high water moved one cabin completely off its foundation.

Scotty Chamberlin tells of his life at Camp Rock Haven:

"I didn't know anything else. I just thought everybody else had that, where you worked day and night. The minute you got up in the morning, like six o'clock in the morning, you were busy until midnight. I thought everybody lived that way."

Camp Rock Haven- top 1948, bottom pre-1948

The Chamberlains developed a dependable business at Camp Rock Haven. They attracted and retained many satisfied customers who enjoyed the attractive riverside camp, the hospitality and the excellent river fishing. The Chamberlains promoted the bass population in the James River by assisting the Missouri Department of Conservation's fish stocking program. Lyle encouraged the Department's employees to stay at Camp Rock Haven. Bass fingerlings were brought to the river in milk cans from the hatchery at Wentworth and carefully released into the James.

During World War II, business slowed due to rationing and the absence of so many men. Scotty's mother was expecting twin sons, Steve and Stan. Lyle took his family to Florida and then Louisiana to find work. He worked for the Higgins Company in Baton Rouge manufacturing landing craft for the war effort. The Chamberlains returned to southern Missouri in 1944. Scotty lived in Carthage for a while, but returned to Camp Rock Haven in 1946.

That same year, the Chamberlains purchased Crabtree Ford farm, a large parcel of land with 5 ½ miles of riverfront within a bend of the James River at Stallions Bluff. The old farm-to- market road crossed the river here, passed Stallions Bluff School and led to Shell Knob. They raised Whiteface and Black Angus cattle and brood sows on the property. The Chamberlains operated the farm and continued to run Camp Rock Haven. Crabtree Ford farm was deeded under a Chamberlain family corporation, Ozark Resorts, Inc. and sub-divided for future development as Hideaway.

Scotty did chores on the farm, trapped mink along the river and worked at the resort. In 1948, Camp Rock Haven was expanded with a motel unit between the house and the cafe. In the post-war era, business picked up as more people traveled and became interested in the recreational opportunities of the Ozarks.

Float fishing flourished and then came the Table Rock project. In the mid-50's, the Corps of Engineers purchased all of Camp Rock Haven and 75% of Hideaway for $62,000. Lyle Chamberlain re-purchased some of the cabins at Rock Haven and moved them to Hideaway. The subdivided lots and 21 cabins became a lakeside development. Some of the cabins relocated to Hideaway were flooded when the lake filled prematurely in 1957, which necessitated moving some of them a second time to higher ground. One of the cabins moved became the home for Scotty and his wife Glenda for 43 years.

Scotty went to school at Joplin Junior College (now Missouri Southern). He and Glenda lived at Hideaway and oversaw the lake-front development. Scotty ran a marine repair shop and taught marine mechanics at Gibson Technical School in Reeds Spring.

Scotty and Glenda Chamberlin built a new home on Stallions Bluff with a panoramic view over Table Rock Lake (Scotty and Glenda passed away recently). The river flows below unseen, where anglers once floated the James, casting for smallmouth before returning to Camp Rock Haven.

Scotty reminisces about his days on the river:

> *"After the lake came in, I fished a little bit, but I kind of lost the desire. It wasn't quite like river fishing. The friendships you made with those kind of people (float clients) would just last the rest of your life."*

William Packwood

William Packwood was born in 1922 and lived with his grandparents in Cape Fair. As a boy, Bill worked with his parents,

Luther Henry and Sarah Adeline, on a farm at Jackson Hollow on the James River. The Packwoods raised milo maize and corn in the bottomland. Bill had eight siblings. Bill recalls the following events of his childhood:

> *"My family lived on the old Carr place at the mouth of Flat Creek in the 1930's and my sister and I would take a johnboat across Flat Creek and walk up to Cape Fair to go to school. I remember one day in the winter or spring when we were using the johnboat to cross Flat Creek and my sister was standing up on the back seat and using a pole to cross Flat Creek. The boat*

66

got stuck on a sand bar and I pulled off my shoes, rolled up my pant legs and got out to give the boat a pull. It threw my sister in the water. There were several tourists on the bank and they really laughed about this. Another time, my father took my sister and me fishing and we tied the boat to a tree and climbed up a bank on Flat Creek and there was a mother skunk with two babies. Our father told us we could catch them and keep them for pets. We caught the two baby skunks, but the mother sprayed us good and when we got to the house, we had to hang our clothes outside. Our father made a cage for the baby skunks and we put saucers of milk in for them to eat. About two weeks later, the mother skunk came at night and dug under the cage and they got away. I lived with my grandfather and grandmother in Cape Fair. They used to take me fishing with them sometimes. We would set trot lines and limb lines and we would camp out on James River and sleep on the gravel bar."

In the late 30's, William's family moved to their uncle Ollie's place at Camp Bear Den near Cape Fair. They had a house moved by wagon up the little creek.

The Packwoods raised tomatoes on the hillsides of Bear Den Hollow. Tomatoes were a common cash crop in the White River Valley during the 1930's-40's. Tomatoes grew well on the rough slopes. Tomato canning factories sprung up all over the Ozarks including Emerson's in Reeds Spring where the Packwoods sold their produce. Tomato growing and processing thrived in the area, but had faded by the time Table Rock Lake came in.

Bill Packwood helped at Camp Bear Den and worked the small farm. He roamed the hills and hollows by foot and horseback. Bill tells about an eerie experience he had on the farm:

"I was walking up home, up Bear Den there and I met these three old gals dressed in white. They just kind of walked right on by me. They were talking to each other. It was as though they couldn't even see me or hear me. And then, a day or two later, I was up on the hill plowing and I looked across the hollow to a trail that went down through there. The same three old gals dressed in white were walking down the hill. They just disappeared.

Then I was riding my horse home from work one night. This sort of a ghost just drifted across in front of my horse. And I thought, 'Well I'm just seeing things.' But pretty quick, the horse started and jumped sideways. So it made me realize I wasn't seeing things- it wasn't my imagination. "

The house at Bear Den burned down when Bill was fifteen. For a while, the Packwoods lived in the barn. Then they moved another house up the hollow and set it amidst the eucalyptus trees. Bill enlisted in the Civilian Conservation Corps (CCC) and was stationed in Idaho. After his CCC service, he went to California. Bill became a successful businessman and now resides with his wife Jean in Salinas. Bill has fished all over the world, but cherishes his memories of fishing the James River with a cane pole the most.

Bill Packwood's father and his grandfather, William Grant Packwood, both worked on the original Cape Fair Bridge. His grandfather, who was half Cherokee, took his wife's name (Packwood) when they were married. Bill's great-grandfather was a full-blooded Cherokee who settled in the Galena area after traveling here on the Trail of Tears.

Ben Loftin

Ben Loftin was born in Barry County and grew up on the family farm at Buttermilk Bay near Carr Ford. He attended school in Reeds Spring. His parents were Lester and Margaret Loftin. In 1948, after serving in the infantry during World War II, Ben and his wife Betty purchased 640 acres at the mouth of the James River. The site was the previous location of the Philibert homestead, one of the first in the area.

The Loftin farm included large areas of fertile bottomland, a natural pond, a high peninsula between the White and James and forested ridgelines. The bottomland was on high terraces that flooded infrequently. With his father and brother, Ben grew corn and hay and ran Herefords on the pastures. The Loftins also raised hogs and kept sheep which they sheared for wool. The livestock were taken to market in Springfield.

There were two access roads to the Loftin farm. One ran northeast along the ridge and connected to the farm-to-market route that ended in Shell Knob (now 39-1). The other road crossed the James River on a substantial bridge and followed the James River Road past Joe Bald to Hwy.13. Ben Loftin says there was a previous bridge at this location that had washed out. In 1956, the existing bridge across the James was also flooded out and never replaced. Ben recalls that trees which had been cut through clearing up the James washed downstream and built up against the bridge during high water. He watched the flotsam piling up against the span until noon. Ben went in for dinner and when he came back out, the bridge was gone. He hadn't heard a sound.

Loftin's cornfield 1955

Loftin's Herefords 1955

Mouth of the James April, 1957

Ben Loftin hunted squirrels and trapped raccoon and mink along the river. He liked to fish at night and especially liked to noodle. Ben knew of many holes along the river that could hold big catfish, flatheads up to 50 pounds.

He would wade into the water and reach up into the holes along the bank. Sometimes he felt a turtle. Sometimes he felt a catfish. He would grab the fish by the gills or use a hayhook to impale the big fish and then drag him out. Ben relates the following story about noodling:

> *"I saw this fish when I was down there noodlin'. The bridge piers had two legs with an open space between the legs down on the bottom of the river. I went down and came around this lower leg. This one fish had his head up against the crossbar. So I came up and asked some of them that was with me if they wanted to go down and look at him. They didn't say anything about going down. I told one of them, 'You hang on to the end of this cord.' I had it tied on to a stick with a hook on it. I said, 'You hold this stick and I'll go down and hook him and you can pull him in.' So I went down and came around this lower leg and there was this big catfish. This little one had dropped down beside him. They were both there on the bottom of the river. So when I came around there, this big one took off. The little one started to follow him, so I just reached out over with the hook and got him in the*

70

mouth and turned him loose. This guy up on the bridge with the cord, instead of him tightin' it up and pullin' on it, he just held it slack. That fish came up, stuck his head up out of the water and broke that pole. That big one went under this big pier from the old bridge. Little Hoss Jennings later on came down there and caught that thing. They weighed him and it weighed 105 pounds. Little Hoss noodled that fish."

Ben recalls that both the James and White could be waded in some places. At the Loftin place, the James ran about eight feet deep. There were some pools along the river that went up to twelve or fourteen feet deep.

Loftin remembers many float fishermen coming by his farm where the two rivers met. Some would stop to get water from his spring.

In 1956, the Loftins were offered $80 an acre for their property which would soon be covered by Table Rock Lake. They took the offer, but were not happy about having to sell. Ben Loftin says, "It makes me mad every time I go down there."

They kept about 135 acres of land above 931 feet elevation, including a few acres on the Joe Bald side. In 1957, the flood took out the house and barn on the old Loftin farm. Ben and Betty bought a farm just off Hwy. 13 south of Reeds Spring and continued to ranch. Ben Loftin ran the contract mail route out of Reeds Spring for several years. He and Betty continued to live on their place, several miles from the river.

Walker Powell

Walker Powell's grandfather, Truman Powell, fought under General Sherman in the Civil War at Bull Run and Manassas as a sharpshooter. He later settled on Fall Creek in Taney County. Truman Powell was one of the first to explore Marvel Cave and was one of the original owners with the Marvel Cave Land & Mining Company. He was a friend of Harold Bell Wright and was the inspiration for the "shepherd" character in *The Shepherd of the Hills*. Truman Powell was the editor of the first newspaper in Stone County.

Truman Powell's son, Waldo Powell, owned a large farm between Hwy. 43 and Big Indian Creek. He operated a steam-powered sawmill on the banks of Big Indian. Waldo was a Missouri State Representative in the 1920's and 1930's. He helped establish the Missouri Highway Patrol and the Missouri Conservation Commission.

Walker Powell was born on the family homestead. The Powells farmed the land on the ridges. They raised corn, cowpeas and tomatoes. They ran Whiteface Herefords, hogs and Angora goats. The Powells hired shearers who used a hand-operated device to shear the mohair. Their livestock was taken to market in Springfield.

Shearing Sheep- Note hand-operated shears

The Powells had a very special feature on their property-Fairy Cave. This large cavern had been discovered by hunters in the late 19th century and showed no sign of previous human exploration. Fairy Cave was opened to the public in 1921 as a tourist attraction. Walker Powell helped his family with the operation of the cave.

As a boy, Walker helped park cars and serve lunch at the attraction. When visitors arrived to tour the cave, Walker would offer them lunch- a dollar for adults and 50¢ for children. He would then help his mother and sister prepare and serve the orders at their home. Fried chicken and biscuits was the usual fare. Walker tells the following story about a lunch incident at Fairy Cave:

"I had a pet bobcat. Wasn't much bigger than a big housecat. He was there at the place, running around the house. I couldn't let him outside, because he'd get the chickens. I tried to keep him away from the table when people were in there, because he liked chicken. One day my sister was taking the chicken back and forth, bringing it out to the table. He caught that swingin' door open and he dashed through there and went up on top of that table. Those people sittin' around that table, they screamed and hollered."

Walker was also a cave tour guide showing tourists the wonders of Fairy Cave. The cavern consists mostly of one huge chamber with spectacular cave formations. The Powell family housed over the entrance and built well-engineered steps and railings inside the cave. Originally, they used gasoline lanterns to guide tours, but later installed electric lighting.

Fairy Cave contains many wonders including the "Cathedral", a massive 85 foot high dripstone formation, unusual draperies, stalactites, stalagmites and many "fairies", combinations of flowstone and coiled and spiraled draperies. There is active water flow in the cave, a small lake and wet passages. The cave contains white salamanders, cave crickets and some bats. Connected to and below Fairy Cave is Mud Cave, which is typically not open to the public. The Powell family sold Fairy Cave to Silver Dollar City in 1971. It is now open as a tourist attraction, Talking Rocks.

Growing up on the farm along what is now Talking Rocks Road, Walker Powell worked the fields, tended the livestock, fished the rivers and trapped the forests. He trapped coyotes, skunks, fox, possum and bobcat. He hunted ducks in the valley up to Neely Spring, the source of Indian Creek. Underground water flowing from Marvel Cave ran clear and steady over a bed of watercress at Neely Spring, now under Table Rock Lake.

Walker liked to float the James and fish for smallmouth and goggle-eye. He and his friends would rent a johnboat at Galena and put in upriver, floating back to Galena for a one day trip.

He also fished for catfish in the White from the shore at night. He remembers the White having holes up to fifteen feet deep during normal flow. There were places the river could be waded at shoals during the summer.

Walker recalls the old wagon trail that ran from the Wilderness Road, past Sow Coon Mountain, above White Rock Bluff and then down to the White River. This trail, once called John Moore Road, crossed the White at Tibbetts Ferry and continued on to Green Forest, Arkansas. Local farmers wanted to improve this trail and in the 1930's, CCC workers developed the road, mostly by hand, as a WPA (Work Projects Administration) project. This road is now DD.

Walker reminisces about the road conditions when he was growing up in the area:

> "I remember my dad was running for state representative. He was going around to these picnics. They had picnics to campaign. He hired a guy up here who had a Model T with no top on it. I was riding in the back. I guess I was about ten years old. So he took me along on this trip to Cape Fair. We had thirteen flats on the way. My dad won the election that year."

In the 1950's, the Powells were offered $15 an acre for a small section of their property on Big Indian Creek. This fifteen acre tract would become part of the Table Rock Project. Walker Powell continued to farm his land on the ridges above Indian Creek and promote Fairy Cave until it was sold in 1971.

Walker and his wife Johanna worked at Silver Dollar City for many years. Walker and Johanna worked as "authentic" characters at the entertainment venue and were featured in television promotions for Silver Dollar City. They resided for many years in a beautiful home overlooking a steep, forested hollow not far from Fairy Cave. Walker Powell passed away in 2017.

Wayne Farwell

Wayne Farwell's great-grandfather Albert Farwell came to the upper White River country in 1858. He purchased and farmed extensive tracts of land along the river near what is now Eagle Rock Park. Over the last century and a half, the Farwell family has continued to work sections of the land on both sides of the White River from Roaring River to Holiday Island.

In 1922, Ola and May Farwell were expecting a baby at their home on the large peninsula of land a mile above the present site of Eagle Rock Park. Ola used their "crank" telephone to call the nearest doctor in Cassville and then headed to the river to assist the physician across the White. Wayne Farwell "arrived" before the doctor did.

Wayne's family farmed the bottomland on what was known as Farwell Bend. They grew corn and ran cattle and hogs on the property. They could cross the White at Lewis Ford near Elm Branch. Calloway Ford was just upriver at Stubblefields. The Farwell Bridge would not be constructed until 1937.

In the early 30's, Wayne's family moved their home to a farm along Route P near the Arkansas border. The road at that time was a rough wagon trail. The Farwells operated a general store at the state line stocked with supplies like flour, salt, meal and coal oil.

Wayne rode the range tending the cattle and worked the corn fields on the land they continued to farm at the Bend. Wayne camped and fished the river. He liked to run trot lines for catfish and float in a johnboat angling for bass. He hunted possum and raccoon and trapped rabbits. Wayne Farwell relates the following treasure story handed down in his family:

"Some men from St. Louis got word of silver hid just across the river from the mouth of Roaring River. This was years and years ago. They found the cave. A bunch of Indians got after them. They had French names. They came down Roaring River. They called it the Smoky River. They found this silver and they were real interested in it. When the Indians got after them, the two men separated. One man hid under a bluff down on the river for a day or more. He figured he'd never get out alive, so he wrote a diary and crammed it down the barrel of his old musket. The last thing he said was, 'Well, here they come. I guess this is it.' They never heard any more from him. His diary showed up in an antique shop in St. Louis. They pulled the paper out of this

gun barrel. We had the diary for several years. That's why we know the names of the men were French. My mother kept that for quite a while. Some true western magazine bought it from my mother and it's gone. We had that diary for several years."

Starting in the 1950's, Wayne Farwell operated a road construction and excavation business. He helped construct an airstrip on the large bottomland on the west side of what is now Holiday Island. The airstrip was under water within a few years. Wayne also cleared trees along the White for speculative land developers.

When the Table Rock Project started, Wayne and other members of the Farwell family lost extensive bottomland acreage to the lake. Wayne has mixed feelings about the lake. The development created economic opportunities for his excavation business, but he hated to lose the "only good crop land" in the area. Wayne opines, "Looking back on it now, I kind of agree with my wife. I wish the old White River was still going down through the willows and sycamores."

Wayne continued to live on his property along Route 23 just south of the Arkansas line.

Esther (Peterson) Hollars

Esther Hollars was born to Jesse James Peterson and Effie Peterson on the family farm in the 1920's. She lived for a few years on the bottomland homestead across the White River from Cow Creek. Her grandfather Benjamin Franklin Rice owned a large parcel of land and operated a store along the river on a side road of John Moore Road (now DD). The Rice Cemetery is still located in this area.

Esther's family moved to a farm just east of what is now Lampe. At this time, around 1930, the location was the intersection of Highways 43 and 86. Esther attended school at the first consolidated school at Blue Eye. Esther's father grew corn on the farm, worked for the Forest Service and for a while,

76

carried the local mail on horseback.

The Peterson family drew their water from a spring by hand. The spring was also used to keep milk and cream fresh. Their home had electricity supplied by a gasoline-powered generator that charged a bank of batteries. The batteries ran lights, a washing machine and a refrigerator. There was no telephone.

Esther married Jay Hollars of Blue Eye and they purchased a farm about a half mile down 86 (now H). Jay was a good farmer. The Hollars ran beef cattle and kept mules. Jay took the best advantage of the ridgeland soil growing corn, burley tobacco, strawberries and tomatoes. Tobacco was dried in their large tobacco barn, formed into "hands" or bales and then taken to market in Weston, Mo. or Kentucky. They hired hands to pick up to 14 acres of strawberries. With a local co-op, the strawberries were crated and hauled to market at the railhead in Reeds Spring. Tomatoes were sold to one of the many local canneries.

Hollars' tobacco barn

Esther Hollars has enjoyed the outdoors her entire life. As a child, she liked to swim and fish in the White River. She remembers the river as flowing fast and clear with pools up to 20 feet deep. With her family, Esther would camp under the stars along the cane breaks at the river's edge. They would fish with poles or trot lines for catfish, bass and panfish. Esther liked to help noodle big flathead and yellow catfish out of holes along the riverbank. She remembers her father catching a mouse while he was plowing. He used the mouse as bait on a limbline and caught a yellow cat between 30 and 40 pounds. Esther says, "There was no better fish than river catfish."

Like most people in the White River Valley, Esther has regularly attended church. The churches of the area served a spiritual and social function. Sunday services often involved big potluck dinners. Sometimes traveling preachers would visit and present spirited sermons for several nights in a row.

Esther relates the following story about a local minister:

"I can tell you about Mrs. Goodwin who lived up Indian Creek. She was a preacher. She built a church up here. They called it the slab church because they let her go to the mill and get slabs. She built the first church house here at Lampe. She would come up the holler with a little lantern hanging on her arm. She was a good preacher. She built that church and then built a bigger one. This was way before the lake."

Esther recalls many tales of the area where she has always lived. Stories of fortune hunters looking for lost Spanish gold on the flat summit of Breadtray Mountain. Stories of the James gang visiting her grandmother Jenny Gallion's place on Joe Bald. (Esther says she is related to the famous outlaw Jesse James.) Stories of a roadhouse on Highway 13 where local ruffians solved their differences.

Esther lived for many years on her homeplace off H Highway where she could view Breadtray Mountain out her window. She continued to fish and enjoyed traveling to New Orleans for Mardi Gras. She was known as a talented painter.

Esther says she liked the river 100 times better than the lake. "Everything good was covered up by the lake," she says. "River fish tasted a lot better than the lake fish- no comparison."

Sanford and Arlene Garland

Sanford Garland was born at home in 1931 near Viola, Missouri to Joseph Theodore Garland and Bernice (Willyard) Garland. Sanford's maternal great-grandfather was Lewis Henry Willyard. In 1891, Lewis homesteaded land along what is now Highway 39 from the present site of Greenshores up to Viola and on both sides of the Kings River. Sanford's maternal grandmother was Olive McKee. The McKees ran a general store and mill in Viola in the late 1800's and early 1900's. The McKee Mill was a large, steam-powered mill that served the region for many years until it burned down.

McKees store was situated just west of the Baptist Church. The church was built in 1884 and still stands today. The stone exterior was added later by Joseph Garland. Grant McKee operated the mill which was located just west of the general store. The mill ran on power supplied from a large steam engine. Water for the steam engine came from a spring behind the mill. This spring still feeds three small consecutive ponds.

Sandy Garland grew up around the family home on Couch Bend (now Greenshores Development) about one mile northwest of Viola. The Couch family also owned property in this area. The Garlands ran dairy and Black Angus cattle on their farm They sold their raw milk to the Pet Milk Company in ten-gallon milk cans, which were picked up daily. If the milk got "blinky" or slightly soured, dairy farmers would sometimes add baking soda to "sweeten" the milk. Sanford's wife Arlene, who grew up in nearby Shell Knob, recalls that the milk company started putting red dye in any slightly soured milk and returned the product to the dairy farmer. Many families would use this dyed milk for personal use. Arlene says, "We grew up thinking cottage cheese was supposed to be pink."

When he was a teenager, Sanford's family moved closer to Viola and he helped at the general store. He roamed the hills and hollows along the Kings River, hunting squirrels and exploring the old bluff shelters along the river. Sanford says, "You could walk across the Kings at the shoals. The water was very clear. We'd ford the river out at the end of the point and climb up to

Couch Spring on Stillhouse Bluff. Sometimes we'd put melons in the spring to keep them cold." (Couch Spring is still visible and flowing today, just above the normal pool elevation of Table Rock Lake at Couch bend.)

Sandy Garland liked to fish the river. He had a johnboat made of pine about twenty feet long and three feet wide in the center, with a squared off bow and stern. The ends of the float boat were tapered in and raked upward. This type of craft was very stable and worked well for gigging. Sandy gigged suckers, catfish and bass from his boat using a long-handled gig.

Sanford's father was the mail carrier out of Viola from 1945 to 1967. Sandy tells of how he had to fill in for his father on one occasion:

> *"Now when I was sixteen years old, I got my driver's license. My mother was seriously ill and was in the hospital in Springfield. My dad stayed up there. You had to be at least eighteen to be a substitute mail carrier. So I couldn't carry the mail. I had a sister who was older than me and she carried the mail. We did that during one of the worst ice storms we've ever had in this part of the country."*

During Sanford's youth, Viola was a thriving little town with two general stores and three churches (including the Baptist and Church of Christ). Like many small towns of the era, Viola had as baseball team. Managed by Doc Kelley, they played teams from other small towns, but never on Sundays. Sandy recalls, "On Sunday, everybody went to church."

Before World War II, Viola had telephone service, but no electricity. The Garlands heated with wood and used kerosene or gasoline lamps for lighting. Water was drawn from a well by hand. Dairy farmers like the Garlands milked by hand until the coming of REA (Rural Electrification Administration) allowed the installation of milking machines.

Arlene (Cooper) Garland recalls the nature of healthcare when she was growing up. "I can remember mother when I got the croup. She'd take a spoonful of sugar and take the wick out of the kerosene lamp and drip some kerosene into that spoon. And I had to swallow that medicine."

Sanford and Arlene Garland were married in 1950. They now reside in the spacious home they built on property west of Shell Knob, once owned by "Wild Bill" Hickok and later by Arlene's family, the Whismans.

Today, there is little evidence of the town of Viola. The Viola Baptist Church is the most visible reminder of the community that once thrived here. But you can imagine where the big mill sat. Perhaps you can visualize the assorted merchandise stacked around the pot-bellied stove at the general store or imagine the crack of a bat as Alan Hale of the Viola baseball team hit a homerun.

McKee Mill at Viola

Wilma (Rice) England

Wilma (Rice) England was born in 1913 and grew up on a substantial farm on Mill Creek just east of Viola. Wilma's parents Derward (D.H.) and Della (Schreiner) Rice owned the property along Mill Creek where it ran into the White River. Wilma's grandfather William Henry Schreiner ran the Schreiner Ferry at Shell Knob.

William Washington Rice emigrated from Kentucky in the late 1800's when his son D.H. was two years old. William built a dog-trot style log cabin above Mill Creek The house consisted

81

of two large individual rooms connected by a passageway. Shortly after the log house was constructed, a two-room frame structure was added at the back, creating an L-shaped home with a dining room and kitchen. D.H. increased the Rice farmland and developed the family business. With three daughters and no sons, Derward often hired help for major farm work. He employed contract crews to thresh and bale hay, cut cordwood and shear sheep.

Wilma's childhood home did not have electricity until about 1949. They used kerosene Aladdin lamps for light. Cooking was done on a wood stove and later, a kerosene stove. With water drawn by hand from the well, laundry was done using a washtub and washboard. White laundry was boiled in a large cast iron kettle placed on top of the wood stove.

Wilma tended the chickens, helped with household chores and went to school at Hideout. She says the school took this name because "it was a little hard to find". As children, Wilma and her younger sister Mabel made the Rice farm their playground.

"My sister and I had playhouses all over the farm. Any field that my dad would be working in, we'd build a playhouse on the edge of the field. When he moved on, we moved on, too. Our dog Fritz was often our companion."

Near the mouth of Mill Creek, there was a bluff shelter that the Rice family visited. Wilma says, "That shelter was our favorite spot. We'd go down and have lunch under there. We had no idea we were treading on graves. My mother would go down and build a fire while my father was working. We would have a picnic."

The Rices grew corn, hay, oats and wheat and ran cattle and sheep on their farm. The mostly cleared farm was fenced and cross-fenced to create pasture and crop land and to separate the cattle from the sheep. There was a large vegetable garden. The livestock were regularly sold at market in Springfield. Much of the farm labor was done with the help of draft horses. D.H. finally bought a tractor in the 1940's. Wilma says, "He thought he should have the biggest tractor made. So he bought this huge one. The thing was so big, I could barely reach the brake pedal."

Prior to 1927, the Rices could cross the White River on the Schreiner Ferry to go to Shell Knob and Cassville. But they most often visited Viola, only a half mile from their home. Wilma's uncle ran the McKee Mill. Viola had a general store that supplied staples, fabric, work shoes and farm supplies. Many items had to be purchased through mail order. Wilma says, "We did a lot of shopping from catalogs- Montgomery Ward, National Cloak and Suit Co., Sears and Roebuck, Chicago Mail Order. That's how we bought our clothes. We didn't get much like that at the local store."

There was a blacksmith shop in Viola for livery and farrier work and of course, the Christian and Baptist Churches. Most rural churches of this era could not afford a full-time preacher. They relied on traveling preachers who would visit every month or so. On the other Sundays, the congregation would hold their own Sunday school.

Wilma recalls that her father spoke of a Viola town band that existed before she was born. Wilma also remembers, as a child and young woman, watching the Viola baseball team play ball. When asked if the girls ever played baseball, Wilma quips, "I remember my older sister Ella batting balls in high heels."

The Rice's neighbors included the Underwoods and the Hoods. Wilma's mother Della held quilting bees. Women would bring pieced tops and stretch them on a large quilting rack Della had at their home. The ladies would work together to quilt the top to the backing. They would sometimes make a friendship quilt with each person supplying a signed and dated square. There were music parties with musicians and singing and square dances held in people's homes.

Wilma Rice attended a two-year high school in Shell Knob. It was common at the time for young people to move to town and board with someone while attending high school. They would spend weekdays at school and return to the farm for the weekend. Wilma finished high school in Blue Eye.

After high school, Wilma married George England. George worked for the U.S. Forest Service and then as a civilian for the U.S. Army at Malden Air Base in southeast Missouri. George moved his family to California in 1946. In 1959, as Table Rock Lake began to cover parts of the Rice property, D.H. and Della sold their farm and moved to Berryville. With their advancing age, the large farm had become too difficult for D.H. to maintain. Wilma says, "My father was a good farmer and manager. My mother was a good manager and housekeeper. It makes me sad to go there now. I remember how it used to be. That was a pretty farm."

Wilma's daughter Ann (England) King spent some time on the Rice farm as a child. She reminisces:

"I was heartbroken when my family left here. I did not want to go to California. I hated leaving my grandmother. I loved it on the farm. I loved the look and smell of the kerosene lamps. I felt very safe there. My grandparents could do or handle anything. I loved the farm. Sometimes we'd walk down to White River. I would wade in the river. I loved to go for a wagon ride."

When much of the Rice farm was buried by Table Rock Lake in 1959, Mill Creek changed from a flowing brook to a large lake cove over a quarter mile wide. The Rice Shelter and the secrets it held were lost forever beneath the lake.

Ann King and her husband Mike purchased a home near the lake in Shell Knob which Wilma and Ann continued to enjoy visiting as often as possible. They appreciate the quiet beauty of the lake and hills, but miss the bucolic life on the Rice farm along Mill Creek.

Wilma Rice England at the Rice farm 1940

Vineta Jane (Terherst) Wingate

Vineta Wingate grew up in the Denver and Enon area. She was born near Denver, Arkansas in 1949. Her parents Glenford Terherst and Nellie (Peden) Terherst share-cropped a farm on Long Creek growing corn and watermelons and raising cattle. The Terhersts had horses, pigs and chickens and a huge vegetable garden. Vineta had seven siblings. She went to elementary school at Farewell.

Vineta did housework, tended her younger sisters and helped with farm chores. There was no electricity at her family's place until 1962. The Terhersts had kerosene lanterns for lights and heated with wood. Milk was kept cool by placing it in a cistern. Later, they had a cookstove and refrigerator fueled by butane. Water was drawn by hand from a drilled well. There was no indoor plumbing. "I never had indoor plumbing until I left home," Vineta relates. "I got married in 1968. My parents still did not have indoor plumbing. When we bought grandpa's farm in 1963, there was a drilled well there with an electric pump. We had power through REA. You had to take your bucket and go out to the little wellhouse, flip the electric switch and hold your bucket there and then carry your bucket into the house." Vineta says they ran water to the kitchen in 1964. Her parents put in a bathroom in 1968. The Terhersts got their first telephone in 1966.

Vineta's family purchased her grandfather Will Terherst's farm near Enon in 1963. They established a substantial dairy cow operation on the mostly cleared rolling hills above Long Creek. Initially, they milked by hand, but purchased electric milking machines by 1964. Milk was stored in a concrete tank and sold to regional wholesalers.

They often used a team of horses and a wagon on the farm. "I can remember going to the cane field and loading a shock of cane into the wagon with the team of horses and feeding it to the cows. My dad always liked to plow the garden behind a team. We got a tractor when we lived at Denver."

Vineta says, "We were busy tryin' to make a livin' to have fun. We went to church and worked and went to school. We went to church about seven days a week. We went to a Pentecostal

85

Church. Sometimes mom and would load us kids up in the trailer and drive the tractor to church. There was a piano at church. Somebody would have an accordion and a guitar." Vineta says for fun, she and her brothers and sisters would scrape "roads" in the barnlot and run up and down the "roads" like they were "cars".

"I lived in the creek. During the summer, we went to Long Creek a lot. Close to our house was a shoal. During the summer, we bathed in the creek. There was a swimming hole. If mom would let us, we'd go to Denver and go to Blue Hole. That was 'the place' to go. It has always been special. Still is today. It was a deep hole about 20 feet deep with a rock wall on one side. Everybody went. It's still a popular place today." (The quality of the stream at Blue Hole has declined recently.)

Vineta recalls fishing for perch in the creek. Her dad fished some; he was usually too busy trying to make a living. Glenford fished for catfish and suckers. He liked to snag suckers in the spring. The suckers were gutted, scaled, sliced and fried. If Glenford brought in a good catch in a 'tow' sack, Nelly would prepare and can the fish. In the winter, the preserved suckers made delicious fish patties.

Mrs. Wingate reminisces, "We canned lots of everything. My father was a good provider for his family. We always had plenty, plenty to eat. My mother was a hard worker and preserved everything. We ate like kings. I didn't know it at the time, but I look back now and nobody was going hungry. Always meat, vegetables, milk, cream, eggs. Our cellar was full of everything. We bought flour, sugar, salt, baking powder and coffee at the general store."

The Terhersts did their doctoring at home. Vineta remembers never having a doctor to their home. Nelly used kerosene as a cure-all. When her brother was bitten on the hand by a copperhead, his hand was placed in kerosene. When the milkman showed up at their place, he took Nelly and her son to Denver and then on to Green Forest where they saw a physician.

Childbirth was assisted by a midwife. Maude Avery was the midwife around Denver for many years. Maude helped deliver

Vineta in 1949, her sister in 1951 and several others after that. Vineta's grandmother Vineta Hopper Peden was a midwife near Enon for several years. She charged two dollars for a delivery. Midwives were required to fill out a birth certificate for each birth and send it to Little Rock. Vineta says, "They were just ladies that knew what they were doing."

In 1955, Glenford Terherst got a job working on Table Rock Dam. He worked as a concrete finisher's helper. He had to join the union and made $1.25- 1.35 an hour. Vineta remembers, "That was good cash money. My father thought he'd died and gone to heaven." Glenford worked long hours on the dam with only an occasional layoff. When Table Rock was completed, he worked on the Beaver Dam project.

"When I grew up there it was quiet. I have pleasant memories as a child near Denver. There was always coming and going and people. Activities. At Enon, as a teenage girl, I felt I was left out. There wasn't anywhere to go. I felt trapped. I was not allowed to get to the world. It was an ideal place, but a 'prison' to a teenager. It was a long ways from nowhere to Enon."

Cemeteries

When the waters of the White River began backing up behind Table Rock Dam, the people in the valleys fled to higher ground. But there were some who could not flee. These were the dead.

The Table Rock Project contracted out the disinterment, moving and reinterment of 1132 graves from 49 burial sites in Missouri and 59 graves from one cemetery in Arkansas. Many of the relocated cemeteries were small with as few as one grave. The largest cemetery relocated was Cedar Valley with 134 sites. Most of the cemetery relocation work was done in 1957.

Cemetery relocation was of course a sensitive issue. The contractors performing the task were required to identify and relocate any items which could possibly be attributed to a burial. Some of the old gravesites were not marked at all and others had uninscribed or illegible markers. Any unmarked graves were reinterred and marked with an "unknown" marker. All existing monuments, fences and markers were relocated.

87

The land containing these cemeteries was seized by condemnation when it could not be purchased outright. Official court documents were filed in Federal District Court naming all the identified grave occupants and their next of kin as defendants in the seizure of cemetery property.

Burial sites located in Taney, Stone and Barry Counties were relocated to eight new or existing nearby cemeteries in Missouri. The only site in Arkansas known to be relocated was Johnson Cemetery which was located near Back Bone Bluff. Of the 59 graves in this cemetery, only one was marked with a concrete monument. The rest were indicated by uninscribed native stones or ground depressions. Little could be found about this site believed to contain burials between 1860 and 1900. Three graves were identified. The gravesites at Johnson Cemetery were relocated to Bowman Cemetery in Stone County, Missouri.

Following is a list of the new cemeteries, the relocation sites and the number of graves reinterred.

Y-Highway Cemetery

Cemetery Relocation

New Cemetery	Relocated	# of Graves
Bowman	Johnson	59
	Jacques Creek	1
	James	1
	Matlock	6
	Vaughn	5
New Bowman	Adam	2
	Beshears	14
	Cantrell	23
	Carpenter	15
	Kedrick	1
Joseph Philibert	Andoe	18
	Cole	7
	Evans	30
	Galaswell	2
	Hale	4
	Hammers	8
	Hardin	18
	Henson	2
	Horn	34
	Leonard	11
	McCord	2
	Morris	23
	Oswalt	14
	Pace	2
	Philibert	97
	Pitts	60
	Thomas	62
	Thompson	6
	Warren	1
	Yates	35
Carney	Martin*	92
Roach	Curry	5
Farwell	No Name*	5
Cedar valley	Ahearn	4
	Geyer	4
	Snowden	17
	Cedar Valley	134
	Oasis	129
New Cape Fair	Carr Ford	19
	Church of Christ	20
	Edwards	11
	Empire	2
	Hershell	2
	Martin*	92
	Miller	35
	Old Cape Fair	40
	Tilden	13
	Wilson	8
	Wooly Creek	23
	No Name*	5
	Packwood	6

Graves at Martin Cemetery were moved to both Carney and New Cape Fair (Y Highway). Five sites in Barry County identified as "No Name" were moved to the Farwell and New Cape Fair graveyards.

In January, 1958, area newspapers reported a scandal involving Table Rock cemetery relocation. Local family members became suspicious in the fall of 1957 that there were inadequate grave removals at the Miller and Martin Cemeteries. When no action was taken on these original concerns, the families checked the supposedly disinterred graves themselves. They discovered remains, artifacts and even a coffin.

Local newspapers (Stone Co. Republican 1-16-58; Aurora Advertiser 1-17-58) reported this misdeed and ran photographs of some of the grave contents. The scandal resulted in an immediate investigation by the Army Corps of Engineers supervising the project.

The contract for removal at these locations had been awarded to an Arkansas funeral director who apparently made only shallow excavations at these sites. When the reinterred graves were examined, they were found to contain only soil. Four graves in Miller Cemetery and one grave in Martin Cemetery were involved. The Corps responded by completely reopening the involved gravesites and properly relocating their contents. They also had all sites that had previously been reported to have no contents reopened. Because of this scandal, the Corps improved contractor specifications and oversight.

Colonel Staunton Brown, Army District Engineer for the Corps over the Table Rock Project since 1954 retired from his position in March, 1958. Considerable pressure was applied on Colonel Brown over the cemetery scandal as well as other concerns regarding project management. The flood of 1957 had raised considerable complaint from local residents about land acquisition, land appraisal, road and bridge replacement and loss of assets.

Unknown marker at Y-Highway Cemetery

When Table Rock Lake was developed, it thrust the people of the upper White River Valley into a different world. Those who lived and farmed in the river bottomlands were the most affected- they lost their land. Finding comparable farms in the area was not easy, but many of these hardy folks stayed and founded new homeplaces and new lives.

With new technologies, more accessible communications and improved transportation, the Ozarks was changing quickly. The Table Rock Project opened up new opportunities and accelerated the tourism trade substantially.

The people whose homes and farms were lost beneath the lake adapted to the new environment. In traditional Ozarks style, they accepted new people and new ways of life, but they also retained their strengths acquired along the flowing rivers and rugged hillsides. And they have kept their memories- their joys and triumphs, their losses and grief, their values and beliefs.

Chapter 4
Natural Features

The Ozarks are ancient. The area that would become the upper White River Valley was covered by a large shallow sea during the Ordovician period 435 to 500 million years ago. Over millennia, the land rose and the sea drained. The Ozark Mountains were uplifted 65 million years ago in the Tertiary time. Forces of erosion carved the Ozark Mountains and created the deep gullies, ravines, hollows and valleys of this area. Water wore away the rock and formed the many streams and rivers of present day northern Arkansas and southern Missouri.

The Ozark Highlands which comprise most of Table Rock's watershed are of the karst type topography. Karst is characterized by thin soils, porous rock layers, caves and sinkholes. Water from the Springfield Plateau and Ozark aquifers, part of the Ozark Plateau aquifer system, rises to the surface in springs which provide the origin for many streams leading to Table Rock. Surface water descends through the porous rock and returns to the aquifers.

Streams which flow turbulently during heavy rains can become intermittent and appear to dry up during dry periods. This constant movement of water through the soft limestone and dolomite of the Ozarks has helped create the numerous caves of this region. Sometimes portions of caves collapse leaving sinkholes and natural bridges.

The White River carved a huge pathway of over 700 miles through the mountainous topography of its watershed. About 60 miles of the river's channel would become the main channel of Table Rock Lake. The White River flowed through miles of rugged hardwood and pine forests. In some areas the river ran deep through quiet pools. In others, it tumbled over rocky shoals. In the broad valleys, the bottomlands contained wide swatches of fertile soil. The alluvial plains contained marshes, shoals and islands providing habitat for numerous species of flora and fauna.

Bear, mountain lion, wolf, elk, deer, buffalo, bobcat, fox, coyote, otter, beaver, muskrat and numerous small mammals and rodents thrived in this riverine environment. The river shores held huge willow and sycamore trees, cane brakes, briar thickets and blocks of tallgrass prairie. Eagles, hawks, turkey, vultures, ducks, geese, herons, ivory-billed woodpeckers, quail and numerous songbirds plied the river valley skies.

The river and its tributaries contained walleye, pickerel, carp, buffalo, suckers, channel, blue, bullhead and flathead catfish, green and longear sunfish, bluegill, drum, eels, longnose, shortnose and alligator gar, black and white crappie, white bass and rock, spotted, smallmouth and largemouth bass. Eels and alligator gar no longer swim in the impounded portions of the White River. A species of small freshwater jellyfish, Craspedacusta sowerbyi, inhabited the rivers. These creatures about the size of a quarter and nearly transparent still roam Table Rock Lake. They are considered to be an indicator of good water quality.

Native minnows in the White River watershed included gizzard shad, bleeding shiner, Ozark minnow, horneyhead chub and several types of darters. Several species of snakes, turtles, frogs, toads and salamanders inhabited the valley. The White was home to several species of crayfish and mussels. Innumerous insects and invertebrates like the hellgrammite resided in and around the water. The caves of the region were home to rare cavefish, salamanders, crawfish and bats.

In 1897, a large pearl was discovered in a mussel shell by Dr. J.H. Meyers on Black River in northern Arkansas. When news of this find spread, people began collecting mussel shells from the area rivers in large quantities, hoping to find pearls. These pearls brought prices of a few cents to several hundred dollars each, depending on size, shape, color and luster. By 1900, collecting freshwater mussel shells for buttons was also found to be profitable. Tons of shells were gathered and shipped down the White River on flatboats. It took about 40 bushels of shells to make one bushel of buttons. Eventually, portable button extractors were used on the upper White to saw out the blank buttons at the site of harvesting. This industry which provided a decent supplemental income to the White River residents continued until about 1940.

Some of the more than a dozen species of mussels found in the White River included hooker-shell, pistol grip, Wabash pigtoe, bleufer, purple pimpleback and bank climber. Mussels were first collected by Native Americans and early settlers for food, utensils and decorative items. Harvesting for pearls and buttons removed huge quantities of mussels from the river. Some people gathered the shells by hand, while more serious harvesters developed mechanical methods. Racks were attached to each side of a boat and four-pronged blunt hooks called "crowsfeet" were suspended from the racks. The boat was maneuvered across mussel beds collecting the shells on the hooks. Today, children still collect mussel shells along the shores of Table Rock. There have been no known reports of pearls being found recently.

The transformation of the upper White River Valley from a riverine environment to a series of reservoirs changed the habitat for many species of plants and animals. Three previously common plants to the river valleys that are now rare are the American beauty berry, yellow wood and switch cane. Cane was particularly thick in the river bottoms, but is now infrequently seen.

Table Rock's rivers and streams were home to many species of small fish called darters. With the tremendous loss of habitat, some darters are now endangered. Although mussels are still common in the lake, some species which require shallow water no longer survive in impounded portions. Similarly, the William's and Meek's crayfish do not survive in the deeper water of the lake.

Henry Rowe Schoolcraft described the vegetation along the James River in the early 1800's as follows,[30] "Along its banks are found extensive bodies of the choicest land, covered by a large growth of forest trees and cane, and interspersed with prairies. Oak, maple, white and black walnut, elm, mulberry, hackberry and sycamore are the common trees and attain a very large size. On the west commences a prairie of unexplored extent, stretching off towards the Osage River, and covered with tall rank grass."

Schoolcraft gave this description of the landscape at the confluence of the James and Finley Rivers:[31] "It is a mixture of forest and plain, of hills and long sloping valleys, where the tall oak forms a striking contrast with the rich foliage of the evergreen cane, or the waving field prairie-grass. It is an assemblage of beautiful groves, and level prairies of river alluvion, and highland precipice, diversified by the devious course of the river, and the distant promontory, forming a scene so novel, yet so harmonious, as to strike the beholder with admiration; and the effect must be greatly heightened, when viewed under the influence of a mild clear atmosphere, and an invigorating sun…".

In the latter part of the nineteenth century, lumbering became widespread in the White River area. The pine forests were almost completely logged out. Oak and cedar were also extensively logged.

Much of the timber cut in the White River region was for railroad ties. The development of railroads in this area had a significant impact. The rails brought people and money into the Ozark hills and were responsible to a large extent for the growth of towns like Branson, Hollister and Reeds Spring. Ultimately, the railroads made this region more accessible to sportsmen and started the growth of tourism. One interesting effect of the logging industry came from a Missouri Supreme Court ruling in Elder v. Delcour. This case found that all Missouri streams are open to canoeing and fishing because they are navigable waters by warrant of their use to float ties.

The lumber industry also had a negative impact on the White River Valley. Removal of the native trees eventually led to a different type of landscape. The pines were largely replaced by oak and cedar. Extensive areas of clear cutting contributed to increased soil erosion and area flooding.

Loading Logs in Reeds Spring

The Cedar Posts Yard- Branson

The hardwood and pine forests of the White River Valley were heavily logged in the late 1800's and early 1900's. As the railroads pushed west and through the Ozarks, there was a huge demand for lumber, particularly for railroad ties. Large tracts were clearcut throughout southern Missouri and northern Arkansas. Between 1910 and 1925, Reeds Spring was the largest supplier of white oak railroad ties in the United States.

Often, cut timber was floated down streams in tie rafts. When hardwoods were removed from the forests and savannahs, cedars often became the dominant tree. Eventually, even cedars were widely harvested for furniture, fence posts and pencils.

Tie hacking was practiced by many local residents as a source of revenue. This was difficult and dangerous work, but helped many families with extra cash income. Oak was the most desired tree for ties and oak was abundant on the verdant hills of the White River.

Hackers would cut trees on their own property and some removed timber from lands deemed "available". Oaks were felled by hand axes and then a cross-cut saw was used to cut the trunk into eight feet lengths, the required size for ties. Wedges were used to split the eight feet logs into suitable sections. These rough-hewn pieces were finished down to the appropriate dimensions, usually six by eight inches, with a broadaxe or adze. A two-man hacking team could produce about ten ties per day.

Finished ties had to be hauled from the forest by horse or mule teams. The railroad ties could then be loaded onto a wagon and driven to town. Buyers marked each tie with an embossed hammer indicating the grade and purchaser. Ties brought prices of $0.25 to $1.00 each. After 1905, when the White River Railroad was completed, ties were sold at any town with a railhead.

Before the railroad came to this area, ties were often floated down the rivers to sites like Cotter, Arkansas. Even after the White River Railroad came to Galena, Reeds Spring and Branson, tie rafting continued as a means to transport the commodity to market.

Cut ties were hauled to the river's edge or in some cases slid down long chutes from the high bluffs. Names like Tie Slide Bluff just above Eagle Rock and Logslide Bluff at Cow Creek testify to this practice.

Once on the water, ties were formed into large rafts and lashed or nailed together. Rafts could be strung together in chain-like fashion with one group attached to the next with a board nailed at each end. This technique allowed the raft to be maneuvered along the river's snaky course.

Hoisting Cedar from the White

Men would ride the rafts with the current, piloting the unwieldy craft with long poles and a rudder on the last section. (see Chapter 6). The tie rafters walked along the raft making every effort to stay in the current and avoid crashing into the shoreline, rocks or other obstacles. Goodspeed wrote, "On June 3 (1874) Francis James and Jack Leonard of the Shell Knob neighborhood, started from the mouth of Kings River with a raft of cedar eighty yards long and twenty-two yards wide. Since 1874 rafting has not been unknown here."[32] When and if the rafters managed to reach their destination, the ties were hauled up out of the river by draft animals or mechanized devices.

By the 1920's, much of the valuable timber in the upper White River Valley had been removed. The demand for railroad ties diminished and tie hacking and rafting ceased to be profitable. Trees as a natural resource had provided a source of income for area residents and helped build the nation's railways. The price paid for this contribution was despoilage of much of the climax forest in the area that would become Table Rock Lake.

The most valuable farmland of the White River Valley was in the bottomlands, but area residents also cleared the uplands to raise tomatoes and strawberries. Farming practices of the early 1900's often called for the periodic burning of cleared areas for use as pasture or cropland.

These conditions contributed to an alteration of the arboreal landscape and led to massive erosion, loss of topsoil and the sedimentation of area streams. Many species of animals like bear, deer and turkey became rare.

To overcome this blight on the land, the Federal and State governments cooperated in forming the Mark Twain National Forest. Thousands of acres were purchased around the White River during the 1930's. This land was replanted or allowed to regenerate naturally. Millions of seedlings were planted by the CCC (Civilian Conservation Corps). CCC camps established in Shell Knob in 1935 and at Roaring River performed much of this work in Stone and Barry Counties. Young men lived in these camps and worked throughout the area planting trees, building and improving roads and fighting fires. Many of the existing structures at Roaring River were built by CCC men. The Shell Knob camp operated until 1941. Some remnants of this camp are still visible today at a community park maintained by the Shell Knob Lions Club at the base of Shell Knob Mountain.

The reforestation of the hills around the White River transformed the area. Although the pine forests and oak savannahs are mostly gone now, the expansive mixed forests are back. And with the forests, the deer, turkey and songbirds have returned. These forests are critical to the maintenance of Table Rock Lake for both aesthetic reasons and to protect water quality.

Only about 5% of the standing timber in the lake bed was cleared during the development of Table Rock. There were two opposing public views on the amount of forest to be removed. People who looked forward to using the lake for boating, skiing, scuba diving and swimming favored removal of all timber. Fishermen and wildlife proponents preferred leaving as many trees as possible. The Corps eventually decided on a policy to remove trees that would remain above water in the main channels. This was primarily on land between elevation 874' and 915'. By following this approach, most of the main lake areas required minimal basin clearing due to the water's depth. Clearing was done down to elevation 840' around planned recreation areas. In many coves and feeder streams, the timber was left in place.

Of course, many areas along the rivers had already been cleared for agriculture at the time of the Table Rock Project. In fact, photographs of some areas prior to the lake show considerably more cleared land than they do today. The forested areas left in Table Rock's lake basin were estimated at 11,000 acres.

Prior to the big dams, when the White River flooded it could devastate everything in its valley. Under normal conditions, the upper White could be forded on foot at numerous locations. Henry Rowe Schoolcraft described fording the White near present-day Lead Hill in his 1818-1819 journal of his exploration of the Ozarks saying,[33] "We lost no time in fording it at a ripple, where the water was only half-leg deep,…". At its deeper stretches, ferries and bridges provided access across the stream. At flood stage, everything in its path was in harm's way. Towns like Branson, Hollister and Forsyth were severely damaged by floods numerous times before the building of the big dams. Those who lived in the flood plain had to be resigned to frequent losses.

The building of Table Rock Lake controlled the flooding and created a new landscape for the upper White River Valley. Many of the natural land formations were buried beneath the lake's water. But there are many clues left which give an indication of what is under the lake.

The course of the White River and its tributaries meandered through some beautiful and interesting country. The rivers careened from one bluff to another, following a tortured path. Sheer rock bluff walls rise where the channel shoulders up against the hard rock hills. The streams curve around long narrow ridges and circle knobs and peaks.

Stallions Bluff 1903

WHITE ROCK BLUFF FROM CAMP YOCUM. JAMES RIVER. GALENA MO. GH HALL PHOTO CO.

White Rock Bluff from Camp Yocum

THE YOCUM FARM
ON THE JAMES RIVER.
VIEW FROM WHITE
ROCK BUFF.
GALENA, MO.
623
HALL PHOTO CO.

Yocum Farm

The James River from Virgin Bluff

The rivers were constantly changing. The meandering flow ran deep through pools, some 20 feet deep or more. Shoals or rapids existed where the water rushed over hard rock. Gravel bars built up at turns and in some places, small islands developed. Sloughs formed behind islands or where secondary channels found a new course during high water. Joy Lee Jones gives the following description of the James River:

"The James River running under the Virgin Bluff was beautiful, but challenging to floaters. Floatfishers first

encountered a beautiful hole of water, very deep and very blue in color. It was referred to as the Virgin Hole. Next was the Virgin Shoal, followed by the Virgin Swirl where the river rushed strongly into a small bluff on the opposite side of the stream from Virgin Bluff. It took knowledge and expertise in boat handling to keep from being swept into the bluff. Boat sinkings were the result of many floaters who were not aware of how to properly guide their boats through these rapids. My grandfather John I. Jones built a fish trap under the Virgin Bluff that provided a resource of food for his family and surrounding families. He had homesteaded land above the Virgin Bluff running east past (what is now) Y Highway."

Virgin Bluff is one of the most spectacular bluffs in the Table Rock area. The sheer rock bluff rises 350 feet above a hairpin turn in the river bed. For millions of years, the river has thrown its force against this massive obstacle- with little apparent effect.

Many stories and legends have arisen from the awesome beauty and power of Virgin Bluff. The name comes from a Native American tale. A local Indian chief's beautiful daughter, Moon Song, fell in love with a young Spanish conquistador journeying through the region. The chief forbade his daughter to marry the white man and in her grief, she threw herself off the bluff into the swirling stream below. The chief placed a curse on Virgin Bluff to keep the white man away. It is also said, Moon Song still haunts the area.

In 1912, a Boston man, William H. Standish, purchased several hundred acres of land in the Virgin Bluff area. He had formulated a plan to construct a reservoir/tunnel type dam

Virgin Bluff was an ideal location for such a project. Standish formed the White River Construction Company and along with Ambersen Hydraulic Company, began a dam project at the site. The plan was to construct a 70 foot high dam across the James at the bluff. At the same time, a tunnel would be bored through the bluff all the way to Winding Stair Bluff downstream. The combination of the dam and long tunnel would produce a tremendous amount of power to a generating station at Winding Stair.

In 1913, Standish began work at Virgin Bluff. A large construction camp was erected in Long Bottoms on the north side of the James. Local men were hired and they began clearing a path up the bluff. Another crew began digging and blasting the tunnel.

George Foster, a local youth, who later became a well-known James River guide, related the following about his work on the project:

> "I got a dandy job there. I was only fourteen years old. I was the water boy. I had a bucket and dipper, would stop at springs and fill the bucket, then make the rounds to all the workmen so they could have drinks.
>
> I got ten cents an hour at first. The workmen on the dam only got fifteen cents. We worked ten hours a day, six days a week." (as quoted in an article by Gerald H. Pipes)

The Virgin Bluff dam project encountered problems from the start. Many men were injured as most of the work was being done by hand with picks, shovels and wheelbarrows. There were landslides on the steep bluff. The tunnelers encountered caves, water and even human bones. Some workers thought they had uncovered the remains of Moon Song. They feared the Virgin Bluff curse and some quit the project.

By the summer of 1913, the threat of world war in Europe diverted finances for the project and the work ceased, never to be resumed. Standish stayed in the area, but was financially ruined.

Other sources have anecdotally reported that there was violent local opposition to the project that would flood the river valley. Locals would sit atop Virgin Bluff and shoot down upon the dynamite wagons, blowing them up. When the dynamite was moved inside the tunnel, disgruntled residents reportedly set it off and collapsed the excavation.

Whether due to the curse of Moon Song, an imminent World War I or the opposition of local residents, the dam project at Virgin Bluff was stopped. The James River was free to run wild, at least for another fifty years.

Virgin Bluff created an exciting path for float fishers on the James. The obstacle produced Virgin Hole where the water pooled, then Virgin Shoals where the stream shot through the narrowed passage, and finally Virgin Swirl where the water eddied dangerously. This section of the river was well-known to floaters and provided both an exciting ride and a campsite on the opposite shore with a spectacular view of Virgin Bluff at sunset. Further down the James was Hicks Rock, a large mid-stream boulder just above Camper's Point. Hick's Rock was both a navigation hazard and a landmark. It also provided a temporary fishing location.

Virgin Bluff still remains a beautiful, awe-inspiring natural feature as it rises above the water of Table Rock Lake. The massive, sheer bluff is a common feature on Table Rock. Only somewhat diminished from their earlier rise above the rivers, these cliffs are named for their color (Yellow), formation (Winding Stair), a local landowner (Stallions), or even their function (Tie Slide).

If you ever boat beneath Virgin Bluff, perhaps you will hear the plaint of Moon Song, or feel the rumble of dynamite, or imagine the rush of a johnboat, craftily maneuvered through Virgin Swirl.

Virgin Bluff & The Rapids

A project very similar to the Virgin Bluff dam and tunnel was also attempted on the Kings River. Known as the Narrows Project, the plan was extensively covered in the Berryville North Arkansas Star newspaper from 1910 to 1912. Joseph R. Neff was the principal promoter of the project.

In 1910, Neff and a group of investors from Springfield, Mo. purchased property known as "the narrows", a thin strip of land at the neck of a horseshoe bend in the Kings River about two miles northeast of Grandview. This was the previous site of Woodruff's Mill. The plan was to bore a tunnel through the narrows and construct a dam on the upstream side of the tunnel. The lake created by the dam would provide a constant source of water flowing through the 225 foot long tunnel with a drop in elevation of eight feet. At the end of the tunnel, a hydro-electric plant was to be built to supply electricity to Springfield. The dam was to be 22 feet high and 300 feet long and was expected to create a lake seven miles long and 400 feet wide. The river's flow would be permanently diverted from "Horseshoe Bend'.

By early 1911, Springfield decided the project was insufficient to supply adequate power and backed out of the scheme. Neff and E.H. Ingram incorporated the North Arkansas Power Company and proposed to supply electrical power to Berryville, Green Forest, Urbanette and Eureka Springs, including Eureka's electric street car system.

By the spring of 1912, the tunnel was about half complete. The North Arkansas Power Company had hired engineers to design the dam and power station and was attempting to sell bonds to finance the project. The scheme never seemed to progress beyond this point.

Joseph Neff continued to live near Berryville until his death in 1937. He was a successful businessman and farmer in the area, but never realized his dream of damming the Kings and providing hydro-electric power to the region.

The Kings continues to flow unabated past the Narrows and through Horseshoe Bend. The only remaining evidence of the Narrows project is a hole bored into the bluff.

There are seventeen islands that exist at normal pool on Table Rock. The largest, Lost Hill Island, at about 100 acres (all land measurements given are estimates at normal pool) is at the confluence of the Kings and White Rivers. Lost Hill is a rounded mound, entirely forested and reported to be the home of numerous deer. It is circled on three sides by Run-A-Round Hollow, a low lying slough that now holds an average lake depth of about twenty feet. The old bridge that crossed the White at this point ran across the extreme western edge of what is now the island.

The northern end of the same bridge emptied onto the shore of Epperly Bluff, what should now be, but is not an island. When the Corps of Engineers develops a project like Table Rock, they are required to purchase all the land within the project's boundaries. Original surveys for the Table Rock project indicated that Epperly Bluff would become an island when the lake level topped the narrow strip of land leading to the peninsula between Mill Creek and the White. Several cabins and homes existed on this property prior to the project's inception, including Riverside Park. To avoid having to purchase all the land and homes at this site, the Corps opted to construct a causeway leading to the peninsula. Many of these homes remain to this day. The portion that would have become an island covers about 70 acres. Along the river's edge at Epperly Bluff existed an unusual rock spire with a hole through it. This formation effected the name Needle's Eye for the peninsula. An alternate story places the Needle's Eye formation across the White near Run-A-Round Hollow. The configuration of the long narrow causeway capped by a wider point has upheld this descriptive name.

Holiday Island is a natural triangular shaped peninsula formed by a large curve in the White River on two sides and Leatherwood Creek on the third side. The 450 acre landmass would be an island if not for the narrow neck of land that connects it to the mainland just east of Beaver, Arkansas. This neck of land, the Narrows, once carried the roadbed for the Missouri and North Arkansas Railroad. Prior to Table Rock, the peninsula was the home of Palisades Farm. The area was reached by a ford across the White River. After the lake came in, the Corps provided funds for the property owner to construct a bridge to the "island". This bridge was the only access to the large peninsula. Starting in 1970, Holiday Island evolved as a large private housing development complete with shopping center, medical clinic, two golf courses and hundreds of homes. The bridge was flooded on numerous occasions when Table Rock reached high levels. In 1990, the span was covered by the lake for seven weeks. Holiday Island property owners had to be ferried across Leatherwood Creek in pontoon boats and then shuttled to their homes in a school bus. In 1994, the Holiday Island developer built a new, higher bridge to Holiday Island with 80% of the expense funded by the Federal Bridge Replacement Program.

Other formations similar to Needle's Eye exist on Table Rock, but they are true islands. On the James, a long point extends out between a sharp bend in the river where it runs into the towering Virgin Bluff. A rocky island of about ten acres exists at the end of the point. The sharp ridge between the island and the north shore of the lake is covered by just enough water to idle a boat over at normal pool.

On Long Creek another island was created where Back Bone Bluff extends out toward the channel. The six acre island is separated from the bluff by a craggy stretch of ridge. Only boats with a shallow draft dare idle across the "Cut". About nine miles up the James, an island of about ten acres huddles fairly close to the south shore. The strait between the island and the shore covers a shallow saddle. Scotty Chamberlin relates a story about a woman whose family once lived on this piece of land:

> "It seems that she and her family were out doing some gardening. She was standing next to a fence and lightning struck and struck her. They couldn't revive her, so they put her in the cistern to keep her cool. They were going to take her in by wagon to Shell Knob for burial. On the way in, she raised up in the wagon and said, 'Where we goin'?' I said, 'Is that story true, I heard about that.' She said, 'Yeah, that was me.'"

The long, sharp ridge is a fairly common feature in Table Rock's basin. The mouth of Rock Creek is nearly blocked by the

1500 foot long Devil's Backbone. This ridgeline extends well out into the lake below the water and is considered hazardous to navigation. A similar formation, the nearly 1200 foot long Hogback, reaches out into Big Indian Creek near Baxter. This narrow, rocky submerged ridge is marked at its end by a warning buoy.

At the mouth of the James River, a long point extends a half mile into the lake bed next to the James' channel. The high point of the ridge is a few feet below Table Rock's surface. This is the historic location of the Loftin archaeological site, the Philibert homestead and cemetery, and the Loftin farm.

Mouth of the James today at lake level 903'

Several other ridgetops, humps and mountain peaks became small islands when the lake was fully impounded. On the James there is a small island mid-lake just above Aunts Creek. A pair of aits in Buttermilk Bay exist as two friendly, wooded islands covering about five and fifteen acres. Elevations above 915 feet extend above Table Rock's surface as small islands of about one acre or less in Jacques Creek next to Indian Point (Jacques Point Island), just off the State Park shoreline, mid-lake west of Clevenger Branch (Breezy Island) and in White's Branch near Kimberling City. Two dots of land rise above the surface just south of the Wolf Pens. Islands of about four acres exist at the mouths of Beardsley Branch (Duck Island) and Clevenger Branch on the Long Creek arm.

Two small islands can be seen to the north from the Long Creek Bridge. The larger island is the top of Goat Hill, the site of the small town of Oasis. The smaller island, where a handful of trees cling tenaciously, is the peak of the slope that rose behind the town.

At lower lake levels, many pieces of land pierce the water's surface- some as small islands, some as shallow points, others as rocky reefs. During extended periods of low water, vegetation will begin to grow on these outcroppings, only to be drowned when the lake rises. Particularly, in the upper reaches of the rivers and creeks, low water can reveal the extremes of elevation and geological formations covered by Table Rock's water.

Powersite Dam was constructed by the Ozark Power and Water Company near Forsyth from 1911 to 1913. Many local residents were employed on the project. Much of the material for the dam was shipped to Branson by train and then floated to the dam site by barge. The large concrete, hydroelectric dam created the largest impounded lake in Missouri at the time. The dam is 75 feet high on its face. Taneycomo is about 50 feet deep at the dam with a surface area of 2080 acres at normal pool of 700 feet above sea level.

Powersite Dam backed up the White River for 22 miles. The dam's gates were first closed on May 9, 1913. Within two days, water was flowing over the top of the dam. Taneycomo was the first in a series of dams on the White River that would forever change the landscape, economics and way of life for this area.

Taneycomo had been an excellent warm-water fishery since Powersite Dam began backing up the White in 1913. Known primarily for its bass and crappie fishing, Taneycomo had attracted anglers for many years. Float fishermen had been plying the White for decades. Branson was often the take-out point for floats on the upper White. Sometimes, floaters fishing on Taneycomo would portage around Powersite Dam and continue their trip down the river.

Table Rock modified Taneycomo in many ways. The water flowing through Table Rock Dam's penstocks and out through the draft tubes enters Taneycomo at a temperature of about 48 degrees F. year-round. This situation forever changed the nature of Lake Taneycomo. The cold water made the small lake mostly unsuitable for bass and other warm water fishes. To remedy this, Taneycomo was converted into a trout lake. To maintain the fishery, Shepherd of the Hills Trout Hatchery was developed on 211 acres just below Table Rock Dam. Rainbow and brown trout reared in the hatchery are stocked regularly into Taneycomo to maintain the population. This fishery has earned a reputation as one of the most popular trout lakes in the country.

The new dam influenced Taneycomo in other ways. Water flow is affected by the amount of releases from Table Rock. These releases, based on electricity needs and lake levels, create variable current conditions on Taneycomo. Due to the constraints of the little lake's size and development along the lake, its level rarely varies more than plus or minus five feet. Recently, historic high water levels on Table Rock have required huge releases of water, resulting in flooding along Taneycomo. The Table Rock releases also affect oxygen concentrations in Taneycomo. These factors are important to the fishery and create considerable interest from those concerned about the little lake's life.

Building White River Dam (Taneycomo)

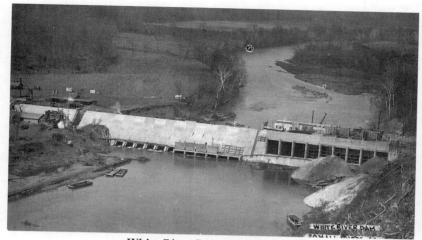

White River Dam (Taneycomo)

Caves, Springs and Treasure

The slopes above the rivers and streams of the White River Valley are pocked with small caves. The karst topography of this area produces many openings throughout the valleys and hollows.

Some of these openings are simple bluff shelters- sculpted by erosion from springs or the partial collapse of bluff walls. Many of these shelters were used as campsites and homes by Native Americans including the Ozark Bluff Dwellers. Shelters were used as hide-outs for bushwackers during the Civil War and shore camps by anglers during the float fishing era.

Small caves dot the bluffs and hillsides in the watershed of Table Rock Lake. Epperly Cave, Hardman Cave, Robber Cave and Magers Cave all contained evidence of prehistoric Native American use. Hardman Cave and Crisp Shelter III had evidence of use in more recent times.

The following letter written by Cloy Brazle to the <u>Knob Rock Rattler </u>newspaper in 1981 describes one cave near Shell Knob. Mr. Brazle was 79 years old when he wrote this account (original spelling):

"I grew up to manhood south of Shell Knob and some cousins and I found a cave near the Turkey Mountain Estates. There was some skelitens, several army rifles inside.

We could not tell about it for we were not supposed to be off the farm. I have talked to a man that lived across the river that watched through a telescope seen men go in and out of this cave he lived in western Kansas.

After the lake was formed I took a professor up the lake in a boat found the cave but the mouth of the cave was filled with a pack rats nest. So we got another boat the next day at the steel bridge at mouth of mill creek took a garden scratcher to dig out the nest but when I started I raked out three snakes (snakes is a birth mark to me) the shelf is less than three feet wide and over a hundred feet down So I quit and I think that I was the last person to be inside that cave and I feel that those skelitons and guns have been hid long enough. The three cousins that were with me are deceased now.

It was 1914 when I was in the cave last. I have read of the cave in two books one called it a robbers hide out and the other book called it a confedart army hide out and Indians may have used it before that.

The cave mouth is the size of a large wash tub the room inside is some 30 ft has a spring inside for their water."

A few larger caves exist along the rivers that form Table Rock. Gentry Cave on the James is an unusual labyrinth of passages. The cave is well-known locally and was a popular attraction during the heyday of the float fishing period. Bear Den Cave was mined for guano as a source of saltpeter and fertilizer in the 1800's. The saltpeter from Bear Den was used in the manufacture of gunpowder by John B. Williams of Cape Fair. The powder mill near the mouth of Flat Creek was the first gunpowder mill west of the Mississippi.

Some unusual cave life was first discovered in Missouri in the late 1800's. Ruth Hoppin of Sarcoxie first identified the Ozark cavefish and the bristly cave crawfish. The grotto salamander was found in Missouri caves in the 1890's. Louella Agnes Owen reported on her journeys into Ozark caves prior to 1900.

Many small shelters and caves were inundated by the waters of Table Rock Lake. Their stories have come to an end. The major caves in the Table Rock area continue to bedazzle visitors with their underground wonders. Two of the best examples are Marvel Cave and Fairy Cave.

Marvel Cave, a large subterranean complex now part of Silver Dollar City, has thrilled people coming to the Ozarks for decades. It is the deepest cave in Missouri at 383 feet. Fairy Cave, now called Talking Rocks Cavern, is an impressive chamber with spectacular cave formations. Both of these caves are directly linked to the geological foundation of Table Rock Lake. The water from Marvel Cave is known to enter the lake at Neely Spring now submerged at the head of North Indian Creek. It is highly likely that Talking Rocks is also hydraulically connected to the lake.

Waldo Powell at Fairy Cave

Treasure

There are numerous legends around Table Rock about buried treasure and lost mines. Some of these troves trace back to the Native Americans, while others are of more recent vintage. A silver mine has been reported near Eagle Rock on what would become the Farwell property. The location is now reportedly under water. Another legend involved Indians and Spanish explorers mining silver at a location on Breadtray Mountain near present day Baxter. If the tale is true, this site would still be on dry land. One story is told of the outlaw Alonzus Hall burying stolen gold coins near the Kimberling Ferry. There have been claims of a wide vein of silver that ran across the White River

115

and could be seen on the riverbed when the water ran clear. Near Reeds Spring, the eccentric Preacher Keith reportedly hid a treasure of California gold in an orchard.

Tales abound and there is some record of men seeking gold and silver at Old Spanish Cave. According to legend, a group of Spanish Conquistadors hid a treasure in the fourteenth room of a many-chambered cave. Over the years, the cave was located and various treasure hunters labored to locate the trove. Collapses in the cavern had sealed off the last fourteenth room and eventually more of the deeper chambers. Some relics were recovered from the cave, but no gold or silver was ever reportedly found.

Perhaps the most famous tale is of the Yocum silver dollars. There is little doubt the Yocums produced silver coins. The location of their source for the precious metal has been sought by many fortune hunters. The mine, if it existed, is generally placed somewhere between Reeds Spring and Joe Bald. A more plausible explanation for the source of the silver is given by Lynn Morrow[34] who suggests the Yocums traded goods with local Indians, were paid in federal coins, and then melted and recast the silver into Yocum silver dollars.

The Ozarks has many tales and legends. When a project the size of Table Rock is built, many historical sites are flooded. It is perhaps this concealment that spawns these stories of buried treasure.

Springs

Integral to the health and life of Table Rock Lake are the springs of this region. Leading up to the modern era, the water table in the White River Valley was higher than it is today. Many more springs existed and their flows were more copious.

The springs of this area were always an attraction to man. Native Americans, pioneers and farmers naturally selected homesites that were near reliable springs. Small springs were used as sources for drinking water and for crude refrigeration. Larger springs were harnessed to power mills- grist mills, sawmills, carding mills and powder mills.

116

Beaver spring today

The spring at Couch Bend today at lake level 910'

Smaller springs existed all along the White River Valley. In addition to domestic and industrial uses, many springs were used for recreation and as a stopping place for those who floated the rivers. Neely Spring at the head of North Indian Creek once supplied the force for a sawmill. Buttermilk Springs on the James was a frequent stop for float fishermen. A spring at Couch Bend on the Kings, now just above Table Rock's surface, was reached by a short climb up a bluff.

The numerous springs of the upper White River Valley continue to supply fresh water, but many of them are now under Table Rock Lake.

Just as Roaring River flows along its course and eventually becomes part of Table Rock Lake, the history of Roaring River is an integral part of Table Rock's story. The Roaring River spring area was settled in the early 19th century and served as a power source for mills as well as a fishery. Goodspeed[35] described the area as follows: "Roaring River rises in a fathomless spring. This is an even flowing well far back in a grotto, whence the waters flow and spread out into a lake. Prior to 1880 a dam was constructed at this point level with the spring. Before the construction of this dam, the waters rushed from the grotto down the rocks with a sound and splash which merited for the stream its name. The lake is a favorite haunt of delicious fish, speckled trout twelve inches long being caught there."

The largest spring in the area, Roaring River Spring is 224 feet deep and flows at an average rate of 20.4 million gallons per day. The water emanates from a cleft in the bluff below Deer Leap at a temperature of 57 degrees.

In 1905, Roland M. Brunner purchased the spring area and developed it into a resort. He built a hotel and cabins and stocked the river with trout from a hatchery he built just below the spring. His development didn't go as well as expected and was eventually offered in a foreclosure sale.

Dr. Thomas M. Sayman purchased the 2400 acre parcel for $105,000 on the Barry County courthouse steps on November 16, 1928. Within three weeks, he donated the property to the state of Missouri. Missouri designated the area Roaring River State Park. During the 1930's, the state and especially the CCC (Civilian Conservation Corps) did extensive development in the park. Many of the buildings, trails and other improvements completed by the CCC are still in use today. During this period, there were two lakes at Roaring River. The upper lake developed by Brunner was washed out in a flood in 1938. The lower "bass lake" was built by the CCC in 1936. It existed until the state drained it in the 60's. Remnants of the lower dam can still be seen today toward the lower end of the park.

Roaring River has been operated as a trout park and hatchery since the early 1930's. Opening day March 1st has always been a very popular event. The excellent trout fishery attracts anglers from around the world. In addition to the clear, cold water this stream contributes to Table Rock, it also acts as a source for rainbow and brown trout. The stream is stocked with about 200,000 trout each year, about half of those raised in the Roaring River hatchery. Some trout released in the park eventually make their way to the reservoir and become part of Table Rock's fishery.

Devil's Pool is one of the geologic oddities of the Ozarks that contribute to the natural beauty and historic lore of the Table Rock Lake area. Located in Big Cedar Hollow just above Long Creek, Devil's Pool was a clear, cold spring emanating from a cleft in the rock walls of the valley before Table Rock was impounded. Originally the spring was about ten feet wide and twenty feet long.

The Native Americans of the area considered the spring a sacred pool with healing powers, calling it Spirit Pool. Early settlers in the region deemed the pool "bottomless" and wondered at the white, blind fish it contained. They named the mysterious, secluded spring Devil's Hole and later, Devil's Pool. The Native Americans visited the site for a cool drink, a bath or spiritual reflection. Early settlers relied on the spring as a water source. Undoubtably, the residents of Oasis were aware of the beautiful, hidden pool and made the short trip up Big Cedar Hollow to enjoy it.

In the 1920's, Harry Worman and Jude Simmons bought the acreage around the site. They both built beautiful summer homes on the property and had a road built to their residences. By the 1930's, erosion on the property and heavy usage of the water reduced the spring's flow. Attempts were made to clear debris from the pool and Worman and Simmons even had a small dam built to contain the water. Drought conditions and continued debris accumulation reduced the pool's flow to a trickle during the 30's.

Harry Worman divorced his young wife Dorothy in 1935. Dorothy later died under mysterious circumstances. Her body was cremated and reportedly her ashes were scattered into Devil's Pool. The vacation homes were seldom used after Dorothy's death and the property was eventually purchased by a logging company. The land was clearcut which led to erosion and additional spoilage of the spring.

Dan Norris bought the Devil's Pool land in 1947 and attempted to restore the spring with limited success. Norris tried to excavate the spring and even poured cement walls around the opening to reinforce the collapsing walls of the rock cleft. Devil's Pool refused to cooperate, running nearly dry during drought conditions and then flowing freely during heavy rains. Locals reported the spring was connected to a long series of sub-surface springs and caves extending south into Arkansas.

Norris developed the property considerably, turning it into Devil's Pool Resort. He built cabins, a swimming pool, horse trails and remodeled the Worman and Simmons houses. In 1958, Norris drilled an 800 foot well on the property and abandoned the spring as a water source. Devil's Pool Resort operated as a resort and dude ranch throughout the fifties. When Table Rock came in, the resort became a popular destination for fishermen. A dock was built and fishing boats were supplied. Several area guides worked out of Devil's Pool including Charlie Campbell, the well-known professional angler. The resort was operated under various owners until 1964.

After 1964, the beautiful Devil's Pool area languished, mostly unused and neglected. Johnny Morris, founder of Bass Pro Shop, purchased the property in 1987. He extensively developed the area, restored the original homes and created Big Cedar Lodge. Today, this first-class resort attracts vacationers and anglers from throughout the country. There are still reports of ghostly images seen on the property- perhaps Dorothy Worman seeking peace at Devil's Pool.

When Table Rock is at a low level, the remains of man's efforts to "improve" Devil's Pool can be seen as rubble at the lake's surface.

Devil's Pool today

Hidden in the deep ravines of Butler Hollow southwest of Eagle Rock is Radium Spring. The spring and associated cave have an interesting and confusing history. The cave was discovered around 1879 by a group of three hunters and their dog. Upon entering the cavern they claimed to have seen "walls which shone like polished silver" and "crystal pillars, light peacock blue in color". Upon leaving the cave, the men were overcome by some illness, resulting in the death of one of them. One of the discoverers of the cave returned to "work" the mine, but a dispute over land ownership led him to abandon the project after he concealed the cavern's opening.

Eventually, word of the cave's wonders spread. James L. Leib, a prospector and self-taught geologist, took rock samples from the cave and had them assayed. Supposedly, the ore contained significant quantities of radium, a radioactive element discovered by the Curies in 1898. The cave and spring emanating from it became known as Radium Cave and Spring.[36]

From the 1920's to the 1950's several entrepreneurs made efforts to collect "radium water" from the spring and radium ore and uranium from the cave. These attempts to extract profitable "radium water" from the spring or uranium from the cave ultimately failed. The positive health effects of radium water were debunked and the mining of uranium was unsuccessful.

It is doubtful that Radium Cave contained extractable uranium. It is more likely that the source of the radioactivity, if it exists at all, is from shale which produces a natural radiation.

Radium Spring has been visited by speleologists and geologists of varying expertise. Reports of Geiger counter readings in the area run from minimal to highly radioactive. Despite the area's interesting and disturbing history, there is no definitive evidence that extractable ore exists there at all.

Deep in Butler Hollow, there are still signs of the attempts to exploit the cave and spring. A National Scenic Byway traverses the area from just south of Eagle Rock to Highway 112. This is a picturesque drive through climax forest with expansive views from the ridgetops. The area is known as Sugar Camp. In years past, local people visited the rough forest to collect sap from the sugar maples. They would camp out for a few days while the sap buckets filled and then boil the product down to maple syrup.

At one time, the Missouri and North Arkansas Railway line ran through Butler Hollow from Seligman to Eureka Springs following Butler Creek through what is now Butler Hollow Glades National Area. In the 1930's, the Federal government purchased large tracts of land in the Sugar Camp area for the Mark Twain National Forest. The Civilian Conservation Corps developed some roads in the forest and erected the Sugar Camp fire tower.

In the spring, Sugar Camp's hills are dappled with flowering serviceberry, redbud and dogwood. In the fall, the hardwood oaks, maples and hickories produce a spectacular display of autumn colors.

Offroad-accessible-only fire roads lead down into Radium Hollow. Along these gutted trails are the signs of past exploration and mining operations. There is a large concrete water tank, a building foundation and a rock bridge which bear testimony to the misguided attempts to extract "riches" from the land.

Cement water tank at Radium Spring

The natural features of the Table Rock basin were indeed altered when the reservoir was constructed. Some plants and animals of the riverways either no longer exist in the area or are rarely seen. Other species have increased their populations around the lake. The spectacular bluffs and alluvial terraces have been subdued by Table Rock's depth. But the vistas of forested hills across the wide expanse of the lake are certainly beautiful. The waters still flow as they have for millennia. The landscape, though altered, is still attractive to many, despite the natural features covered by Table Rock Lake.

Crossing White River

Chapter 5
Fords, Ferries and Camps

The first people who migrated into the White River Valley near the end of the last ice age were probably following big game- mastodon, giant buffalo and giant beaver. Game trails led over the uplands, through the savannahs and across the streams and rivers. The rivers were waded at fords. The best fords were usually at shoals where the water was relatively shallow and the bottom rocky. Native Americans probably used dugout canoes or rafts to cross at some locations, although there is little evidence of this until the historic period.

When European settlers began populating the area, many homesteads were established at advantageous locations along the rivers. These locations were at the confluence of two water courses, promising sites for water mills or reliable fords. Henry Rowe Schoolcraft[37] described fording the White near present-day Lead Hill, Arkansas in the 1818-1819 journal of his exploration of the Ozarks saying, "We lost no time in fording it at a ripple, where the water was only half-leg deep,..."

There were many fords across the White, the James, the Kings and the other tributaries that would become Table Rock Lake. Some became crossings for major market routes and eventually required ferries. A few became the sites for bridges. Many fords were just convenient crossings for local residents or a means for landowners to reach their property on both sides of the river.

Area streams often provided a convenient route for roads. The relatively flat and open bottomlands along creeks were suitable for rough travel routes. The meandering courses did necessitate frequent fords on these roads.

Prior to Table Rock, a series of unimproved roads followed Long Creek, including numerous fords, between Oasis and Enon. Aunts Creek School was along a route that forded Aunts Creek in several places. Flat Creek was crossed by fords in many locations including Wilson, Henson and Carney Fords. Local farmers drove cattle along a rugged road paralleling Roaring River. This trail forded the stream often before picking up the old Roaring River Road on its way to railheads at Cassville and Exeter.

Generally, there were many more fords on the smaller streams and the upper reaches of the rivers. Below the Kimberling crossing, the White became too wide and deep to be practical for fording. There certainly were areas along the river that could be forded, particularly at low water levels, but these crossings were unreliable for consistent use. Some fords were improved to paved low-water crossings in the first half of the 20th century. Where fords were impractical, ferries were employed. Eventually, the major routes required bridges.

Fords prior to the lake on Long Creek existed at Enon, Backbone Bluff, the mouth of Clevenger Branch and near the present-day site of the State Park Island. There were also crossings beneath today's Long Creek Bridge.

Up the White, Skelton Ford crossed above Beaver Town. The only access to Palisades Farm (today's Holiday Island) was a ford over the White. Further down the river were Calloway, Lewis, Easley and Cotner Fords. Smith Ford was near the present site of Sans Souci. There was Morris Ford at Epperly Bluff where the old Shell Knob Bridge would be built and a ford where the new Shell Knob Bridge is located. Big Creek could be forded at two sites- one just above the White and the other at the present site of Big Bay Park. Andoe and Arnold Fords crossed the White in the Owens Bend area.

Many fords existed on the James River. Just above the White, a ford crossed to the Philibert farmstead. This ford was eventually improved to a bridge. Three miles up the James was Oswalt Ford followed by Stewart Ford above Aunts Creek and the Carr crossing at Buttermilk Springs. Just below Piney Creek, the James was forded by a route leading to Martin cemetery and Piney Creek School. Above Piney Creek, Wilson, Cole and Hanes Fords crossed the river. Melton and Miller Fords provided access to Miller cemetery and Cape Fair. Before reaching Galena, local access across the James was at Lower Stone Ford and a crossing at Carr Bottoms.

The Kings River was forded just below the location of the present 86 bridge at Prentice Ford, near Sweet Water Branch at Garrison Ford and at the mouth of Gamblers Gulch, Viola Ford.

The river fords were critical to the development of the White River Valley. In ways, the White was the lifeblood of the area, but it was also a barrier and could even be a destroyer. As the upper White River area was settled in the 1800's, the need for more reliable river crossings became necessary. Ferries were established at several major points on the rivers.

Ferries

The Wilderness Road crossed the White at what is today Kimberling City. A ferry began operation here as early as 1847. The crossing was run by Mayberry and over the next several years, Saber, Allen and Smith. William Kimberling and Henry Thomas purchased the ferry in 1870. Kimberling ran the river crossing until 1922 when the first Kimberling Bridge was built.

Ferry operation was licensed by the county and regulated by the state. There was an annual fee to receive an operating permit. Kimberling built a new ferry about every five years. The christening and launching of a new craft was a major community event. The guide cables were replaced annually. Kimberling lived on the south side of the river and raised a family of fourteen children. It has been reported that the fees for crossing the White River were 50 cents for a wagon and team, 25 cents for a horse and buggy and 10 cents for a person on foot.

Other ferries that operated on the White were Beaver's Ferry at Beaver Town, Lewis Ferry above Roaring River, Golden Ferry at the present site of Big M, Painter, Morris and Prentice Ferries at the mouth of the Kings River where Alfred Painter received a license to operate in 1872, Schreiner Ferry at Shell Knob, Coombs Ferry at Indian Creek and Tibbetts Ferry at Cow Creek. A ferry also crossed the James at Galena. In 1860, Green B. Easley was licensed to operate a ferry on the White River just above Roaring River. This site was a river ford along an old road which ran between Cassville, Missouri and Carrolton,

Arkansas. The Easley farm was situated within a large bend of Roaring River where the stream met the White.

River ferries were generally simple craft, but they had to be solidly built. Ferries transported pedestrians, wagons, livestock and supplies. They had to withstand constant pressure from the river current and frequent beachings. Ferries were rebuilt or replaced every few years. Ferrymen often kept a rowboat or johnboat at the ferry site to transport individuals or small groups of people across the river.

A typical ferry was constructed of hardwood lumber and was generally about 40 feet long. Basically a raft, a ferry had heavy gunwales or sides and plank decking. A ramp which could be raised and lowered was attached at each end. There was usually some type of railing along the sides.

Compton Ferry- Branson

The Hawkins Ferry- White River

128

A heavy metal cable was strung across the river several feet above the stream attached to large trees or heavy posts on either side. Another cable ran from each end of the ferry up to a pulley which slid along the main cable. Each end of the ferry cable was attached to a windlass. The ferry operator turned the windlass which wound the ferry cable from one end or the other. Winding the cable turned one end of the ferry upstream and one end downstream. The ferry was pushed off from shore and the current would catch the downstream end and move the craft across the river along the main cable. To cross back, the ferry was repositioned with the opposite end downstream. Under normal conditions, the river current was the only means of power necessary. In some cases, long poles were used to propel ferries across the water.

Ferrying was dangerous work. Most ferries would not operate under flood conditions, but the need was great to keep traffic moving, so ferrymen often needed to cross even with high water. Heavy, shifting loads, variable currents and water levels and floating debris were all hazards to ferry crossings.

The family of Tim Loftis knows well the dangers of ferrying. Tim's great-grandfather Henry Schreiner bought the old Morris split-log ferry in the late nineteenth century. Henry ran a cable ferry service across the White River very close to the present site of the Shell Knob Bridge.

The Schreiners (different spellings are used) had a homestead on the south bank of the White about two miles east of the Kings River (this site is now the location of Knob Hill Acres). The Schreiners had a log home on the high terrace above the river. In 1927, they built a new home farther up the hill.

A rough wagon trail traveled along what is now 39 Hwy. to the Schreiner place. The ferry road ran down a draw and along Hidden Cove out to the river. The Schreiner cable ferry crossed the White depositing passengers on the north shore where the trail ran up High Dive and on to Shell Knob.

When Henry Schreiner died in 1898, his two sons Frank and Bill continued the family business. On June 25, 1915, Lewis and Henry Schreiner drowned at the ferry crossing. The <u>Cassville </u>

Republican reported on July 8, 1915, "The body of Lewis Schreiner, the 12 year old son of Mr. and Mrs. Frank Schreiner, and one of the two boys who were drowned Friday, June 25 at the Schreiner ferry near Shell Knob, was found Friday July 2 about 8 miles below the ferry."

Frank Schreiner was broken hearted over the drowning and quit the ferry business. His brother Bill continued to run the crossing. Frank oversaw the family farm, growing corn and hay in the bottomland and running cattle. Frank's daughter Stella married James Eric Loftis and the couple helped with the family business. On April 15, 1927, James drowned in the White River when the stream ran at flood stage. Six months later, his son Tim was born. The loss of James Loftis and the construction of the White River Bridge in 1927 put an end to the ferry service in Shell Knob.

Over the next several years, Tim Loftis spent time in Arkansas and at the family farm in Shell Knob. He remembers their home having kerosene lamps and drawing water by hand from a drilled well. They had a party-line telephone. He would visit Charlie Burris' home and listen to a battery operated radio. Tim made trips to Hardman Cave on the Tom Hardman property which adjoined the Schreiner farm. And he could gaze off down to the river where the old ferry lay abandoned, partially covered with gravel, conjuring thoughts of what had been.

Tim's uncle Elmer continued to run the Schreiner farm. Elmer's son Edgar grew up on the place. Edgar recalls growing corn, hay and oats on the bottomland property. Crops were often not planted until June to avoid losses from flooding. The Schreiner's crops were mainly used to support their dairy and beef cattle operation.

The land was worked with a 1945 Farmall tractor. Hay and oats were harvested with a binder. Corn was picked by hand. The Schreiner's livestock were housed in a 40'x60' barn. Edgar's mother maintained a vegetable garden and laying hens. Most everything they needed was produced on the farm.

Edgar remembers occasional trips to the general store in Shell Knob or Viola for basic supplies. He heard many stories told on the front porch of Whisman store in Shell Knob. Edgar relates the following tale:

> *"Doc Salyers had a horse named 'Ball'. Doc was proud of that horse and liked to brag on how smart that horse was. On one of his doctoring trips, Ball lost one of his shoes. So, Doc brought the horse into town and left him untethered. Ball walked on over to the blacksmith shop run by Perry Epperly. Epperly looked at that horse. Ball looked at Epperly. One of the locals watching this scene said, 'Doc, what're they waitin' fer?' Doc said, 'Ole Perry's waiting for Ball to show him which foot needs a new shoe.'"*

Edgar lived on the farm until his father Elmer had to sell it for the Table Rock project. The property sold for less than $40 an acre. They received a small concession for crops lost in the flood of 1957. Edgar's folks bought a farm near Jenkins where Edgar continues to work and live today. Edgar retains a length of the cable ferry his grandfather used to guide the Schreiner ferry across the White River.

Tim Loftis currently resides in Green Forest, Arkansas and frequently visits Shell Knob and Viola. He cherishes his memories of this area, but reminisces poignantly, "My mother had two brothers drown, her husband drowned and her grandson." The Schreiner family truly made sacrifices in their efforts to tame the White River.

River ferries were the major means of crossing the White along the most important routes until the early 1900's when wagon bridges and later automobile bridges were constructed. By the 1930's there were very few ferries in operation on the upper White. However, during construction of the Table Rock Project, ferries were used when the lake rose before some of the lake bridges were completed. Army personnel operated a ferry at the Kimberling Bridge construction site in 1957. At many other crossings like Eagle Rock and Shell Knob, local residents had to use boats to cross the lake before the bridges were completed.

Camps

Even before Table Rock Lake finally filled in 1958, the rivers of the area provided a wealth of recreational opportunities. Just about everyone who lived near the streams swam in them. All the individuals interviewed for this book who lived in the area before Table Rock reported swimming in the streams.

Many of the river crossings were also popular camping locations. Campsites originally developed at these crossings when travelers had to wait for suitable water conditions. Particularly during flooding, those who wished to ford or ferry the river might have to wait days for a safe crossing. Campsites developed naturally at places like Eagle Rock, Shell Knob, Cape Fair and Kimberling.

During the float fishing era, many camps were established along the rivers, particularly on the James. Some camps were simply a convenient sand bar with good tent sites. Other camps developed into established resorts with cabins and amenities for long-term family vacations.

Camp Yocum From White Rock Bluff

Camp Look Out

Float trips started in the Ozarks around the turn of the century. Visitors to the area's spas and springs were attracted by the many fine float streams and the great fishing. The event that probably first widely publicized float fishing in the Ozarks was an excursion on the Current River organized for Missouri Governor Herbert S. Hadley in 1909. A photograph of the party at Round Spring was widely publicized and drew national attention to the sport and this area.

Harold Bell Wright, the author of *The Shepherd of the Hills,* made at least two float trips in the early 1900's- one from Galena to Branson of about a week and another longer trip. He apparently did little fishing, but may have received some inspiration for his well known books.[38]

Charlie Barnes of Galena is usually credited with creating the first johnboat in this area. He modified a gigging boat by shortening and widening it. The boats were mostly built from pine, but redwood and cedar were also used when available. These craft were 20 feet long and about 30 inches wide. Some boats used on the upper White were narrower.

Charlie, Herb and John Barnes started one of the area's first commercial float fishing operations in the early 1900's.

133

In addition to building boats, they guided five-day trips on the James and White River from Galena to Branson. Charlie later built boats and also guided for Owen Boat Line.

Jim Owen, owner of the Owen Boat Line out of Branson, Missouri, is probably most responsible for publicizing and popularizing float fishing on the upper White River. Starting in the 30's, Owen ran seasonal floats almost daily on the James, upper White, Kings and Buffalo Rivers. Floats could start near Galena on the James or Eagle Rock, Shell Knob or the Kimberling crossing on the White.

The Owen Boat Line primarily catered to affluent anglers from cities of the midwest, but also guided many celebrities of the era. These anglers were serious fishermen and used the best tackle of the day. Most fished with casting rods and baitcaster reels like Shakespeare, Langley and Pfleuger. They used artificial lures like the BassOreno, Peck's Bait, Lazy Ike, Flatfish, River Runt and Hawaiian Wiggler. These fishermen (and sometimes women) caught lots of smallmouth and largemouth bass. They also took goggle-eye, catfish, walleye (jack salmon) and even eels.

Owen's johnboats were built by Charlie Barnes of Galena. They were 20 feet long, about 30 inches wide and made of pine with metal ribs, usually with a seat in the back for the guide. Clients sat in deck chairs placed in the boats. Some of these craft had a false bottom to keep equipment and feet dry. These floats were always guided by a local man who worked for a daily rate and tips. The guide steered the johnboat with a wooden paddle. They also set up camp, cooked and gave fishing advice. Many float trips included a commissary boat.

Giggers c.1900 The original caption reads, "Picture taken about 1900-residents of Galena where commercial float fishing originated. "Giggers" say they don't like anything but rough fish (not game fish) to eat, feeling it was tastiest, but old timers (as shown) went for game fish."

Early fishermen

In the days before the big reservoirs, float trips lasted several days. Many floats would end at Taneycomo, but some continued down the White into Arkansas. At the end of a trip, boats and equipment were shipped back to Branson and Galena by truck or railroad.

Buster Tilden of Galena was a guide for Jim Owen in the 40's and 50's. He floated many trips on the James and White and some on the Buffalo in Arkansas. Some of his floats started as high up the James as the mouth of the Finley. Others started several miles up Flat Creek. Many of these trips ended on Taneycomo where the guide would often use a small outboard to make the final run into Branson. Some guides would stay over in Branson at Owen's bunkhouse.

Buster's guiding started in May when the stream bass season opened and ran into the fall. He floated with clients from all over the country including Springfieldians Ralph Foster and Bill Ring of KWTO radio. Most of these anglers used good quality equipment. Shakespeare and Pfleuger baitcasting reels on aluminum, steel or fiberglass rods were common. A few liked to fly fish for bream. Others enjoyed trot lining at night. Many guides discouraged trot lining due to the extra work involved. When live bait was desired, glass minnow traps were placed in the stream to acquire baitfish.

Most of the float anglers used artificial lures like the Crippled Minnow, SOS or Peck's Bait. Tilden's biggest bass, a 7 pound largemouth came out of the James on a Peck's Bait. He relates a story about this large horsehair jig with a small spinner attached at the head. One of Buster's fellow guides liked to drink. On one occasion, this guide told his clients that they'd have to give him a snort of their liquor every time they got hung up. The prideful anglers took up the challenge and then proceeded to take their guide's advice to fish a Peck's Bait really slow. The heavy, large-hook lure provided several shots for the guide that day.

The float guide's day was a long one involving loading equipment, steering the johnboat, giving fishing advice, cooking meals and setting up camps. Larger floats often had a commissary boat hauling equipment and supplies. The commissary man would float ahead of the others and set up the lunch and overnight camps on gravel bars. There were many established camps along the river routes. In addition to the guide and angler clients, the johnboats carried wooden camp boxes, ice boxes with large blocks of ice, tackle, food and water jugs. Guides were typically paid $4-$5 a day plus tips.

The fishing in these streams was for largemouth and smallmouth bass, walleye, catfish and suckers. Fish were often eaten on the trip, but seldom taken home.

Buster Tilden fondly remembers his days on the river before Table Rock. He is proud that he only sunk his johnboat once. Flat Creek was a fast flowing stream and Buster was guiding a client who had only one leg. Trying to push his boat past a snag, the johnboat turned sideways and filled with water. His client only lost his lunch and a couple of bottles of beer, but he was hopping mad.

The first half of the 20th century saw extensive float fishing in the upper White River basin. In addition to the Barnes' and Owen's operations, Bill Rogers and Lyle Chamberlain outfitted float fishing excursions. Other names associated with the industry were Yocum, Long, Stewart, Dillard, Hemphill and Melton. For several years, Galena was known as the "Float Capital of the World". Float fishing had a sizable economic impact on the area through employment and the sale of goods. It attracted visitors from all over the country including movie stars, politicians and national sports writers. The enjoyment and fishing success these clients experienced added to the considerable popularity of the upper White River basin as a desirable destination for angling and vacationing.

After Bull Shoals was completed in 1951, floats were primarily on the James and upper White above Branson. When Table Rock was finished in 1958, the era of the big float trips began to wane. Some outfitters continued to operate on the upper James while others like J.D. Fletcher floated the White and Kings in Arkansas.

Anglers at Jackson Hollow early 1950's

Hicks Rock at Campers Point on the James

Lyle and Alma Chamberlain and their son Scotty operated Camp Rock Haven on the James at Cape Fair from 1930 to the mid-50's. The camp was on the original site of the Aurora Fishing Clubhouse. Camp Rock Haven was popular with serious anglers, couples and families. The cabins and amenities at the resort provided services to many people before Table Rock Lake was completed. Camp Rock Haven was able to approach float fishing differently than some of the other outfitters. They specialized in one day floats. Fishermen were put on the river at Cape Fair for a day's float to Cole Ford. The Chamberlains picked up their clients and shuttled them back to Camp Rock Haven where they were fed at the Fisherman's Hat Cafe and relaxed for the evening in the cabins. The second day would involve a float from Cole Ford to Stallions Bluff. The third float would be from Stallions to Bill Roger's camp at the Kimberling Bridge.

Scotty Chamberlin relates the story behind the Fisherman's Hat Cafe's name:

> *"The customers would leave their favorite fishing hats with their favorite fishing lures on the walls of the cafe. When returning, they would don their hats and declare their desire to 'hit the river'. The cafe was the local hangout for the guides in hopes of picking up a stray guide job. One evening, Dad mentioned he had bought some white grapes and they would probably get rotten before they were sold. The next day, one of the guides came into the café with a nice stringer of fish. When asked, 'What did you catch them on?' he retorted, 'White grapes!' Needless to say, Dad sold all of the white grapes."*

Chamberlain's float service involved a lot of shuttling. Early on, Jack Melton and Walter Hardin hauled johnboats for Camp Rock Haven. Later, Scotty Chamberlin drove the shuttle truck. Scotty relates that typically the boats were placed on the flat- bed, the deck chairs and equipment were placed in the boats and the float clients sat in the deck chairs for the bumpy ride back to camp. Some of the wealthier customers would have their own cars shuttled to the take-out site for a slightly more comfortable ride back.

Camp Rock Haven employed several local guides. Some of the guides who worked for Chamberlain were Henry Bob, George, Ott and Dean Byrom, Junior Pace, Eldon and Waldo Haynes, George Foster, Henry Crabtree, and Clyde, Edward (Skip) and Harold Dean (Peanut) Carr.

The guides were in charge on the water. They were responsible for the equipment and safety of their clients, successful fishing and most camp duties. Chamberlain's guides started out at $3 a day and later were paid $5 to $6 plus tips. A typical tip was $5 per day. Chamberlain occasionally floated Flat Creek. He also outfitted trips to the Current and Gasconade to keep his guides busy.

Scotty Chamberlin relates the following information about float fishing at Camp Rock Haven:

"Some of our customers enjoyed floating by the light of the moon. Jitterbugs were our choice of lures. No matter the size of the fish that slapped the lure, it sounded like a whale and your heart skipped a beat or two.

Jack Melton of Blue Haven Camp and his guides' choice was the Crazy-Crawler with two loose metal spoons on the sides. Rock Haven and Blue Haven guides would have friendly competitions during non-busy times.

Frogging floats were also a favorite pastime. Some used a short handled gig, some used a rod with a hooked fly and Dad relied on catching them by hand when he and Mom would float alone.

Our giggers were a bit more modern in their lighting. They used a modified white pressurized gas lamp with four double mantles and a 20 inch curved reflector. You could see them coming for a mile or more.

I also remember Buster Tilden's one-legged guy. I about had a heart attack when Dad told me to drive a car to Cole's Ford, I got in and saw the artificial leg leaning on the front seat. I always wondered why the guy started asking for George Byrom instead of Buster, now I know. I was taught at an early age to not ask questions and not to speak unless spoken to.

Not that it matters much now, but Dad and Marlin Perkins were camping buddies all through school in Carthage, Mo. My grandmother would take them to Spring River or Shoal Creek for several years when they were young. They were both "outdoorsmen". Dad supplied many specimens sent to the St. Louis Zoo. Their last visit I am aware of was when Marlin and some money backers bought the Marvel Cave about 1953. Now it's Silver Dollar City."

In the early 1950's, a single cabin at Camp Rock Haven rented for $2.50 per day or $15 per week. The cabins included a hot plate for cooking, dishes, kitchen utensils and bedding.

Many customers brought their families to the camp. While the men fished, the women and children enjoyed the peaceful campsite on the river.

Camp Rock Haven was flooded several times by the James River. After each such event, the Chamberlains had to thoroughly clean and repair their facilities. When Table Rock Lake came, Camp Rock Haven was sold to the Corps. Several of the cabins were moved downriver to Hideaway on Stallions Bluff where the Chamberlains owned a large farm. Some of these cabins became vacation homes. Scotty and Glenda Chamberlin lived in one of the cabins for 43 years.

Guides at Camp Rock Haven, left to right: Harold Dean
(Peanut) Carr, George Foster, Edward (Skip) Carr

Camp Rock Haven torn down 1958

Moving cabin from Rock Haven to Hideaway

Bear Den Camp was operated by Ollie Packwood from the late 1930's until the lake was filled. It was located at the mouth of Bear Den (sometimes spelled Bearden) Hollow on the banks of the James. Camp Rock Haven was right across the river. A farm-to-market road came up from the south, ran right next to Bear Den Camp and then paralleled the river bank before meeting 148 at the east end of the old Cape Fair Bridge. The route was a one-lane gravel road.

Bear Den had cabins for rent and a camping area. Packwood rented johnboats and outfitted float fishermen. Anglers coming to Bear Den could arrange short one day floats or longer trips to as far as Branson.

Ollie Packwood sold the Bear Den Camp property to the Corps. When the lake first filled in 1957, the buildings were destroyed by the rising water.

There were many other camps and resorts along the James before Table Rock. Several commercial fishing camps were established on the river in the early 1900's. Among these were

Limberlost, Long Camp, Sleepy Hollow Camp and Taylor Camp. Camp Yocum was located about three miles above Galena on a wide curve in the James. The camp was operated by the family of Tom Yocum, one of the most accomplished float fishing guides on the river.

The following description comes from a brochure circa 1922:

"Arnold Lodge is the oldest and best camp on James River. 2 ¼ miles from railroad station at Galena, on a large farm, where you can get fresh milk and butter delivered at camp every day, where the best melons and cantaloupes in the country grow. It is handy to reach with cars, as it is on a good road, and is only 150 feet from the water's edge on the beautiful James River in a grove of native oak, maple and walnut shade trees. You can sit on your porch and look down the river and watch the bathing and fishing, see the bluffs and observe nature all the day long, and at night when the moon creeps over the hills you can look over the glimmering water and forget your crowded little office at home. You take a walk one half mile through the woods to the Gentry Cave that winds through the hill with its wonderful sights. Those that want to bring their families and leave them in camp- may do so, and take a boat and make the haul overland, a two-hour's drive, to the mouth of Crane Creek, and a good day's float back to camp. You can also make the eight mile float down the river to the Carr Ford, and haul back only two miles to camp. There are many other floats you can make if you wish, with the black bass fishing the best in the Southwest. All you need to bring is your personal bedding. You can buy your provisions at Galena."

Over the years, local fishermen and float guides established many temporary camps along the river. These camps were used as convenient places for shore lunches or overnight camping. The best camps were on islands, terraces or gravel bars with reasonably level terrain. A good spring for drinking water was a plus. Some camps were set-up at fords or near roads to facilitate putting in and taking out the boats.

Some of the camps starting at Galena and traveling downstream were Mack Spring Hollow, Tilden Hole, McCord Bend, Rogue Ford, Carr Bottoms, Stone Ford and Jenkins Ford.

Mash Hollow where Flat Creek met the James was reputed to be a stop for white lightning. At Cape Fair was Camp Rock Haven with Log Cabin Camp next door. Across the river was Bear Den Camp operated by Ollie Packwood.

After passing Cape Fair, floaters could stop at Swift Hole, Virgin Bluff, Miller Springs, Hoppy Gravel Bar, Long Ben Bluff, Cole Ford, Winding Bluff and Campers Point. Campers Point was just below Hicks Rock, a well-known landmark where the river split around a large mid-stream boulder. At Buttermilk Springs, float fishermen could beach their johnboats and walk up the hollow where cold spring water and chilled buttermilk were available for a quarter.

Continuing on down the widening stream, there were stopping places at Crabtree Hollow, Nolen Hollow, Winding Stairs, Jackson Hollow (Creller Camp), Aunts Creek and finally Naked Joe Bald before the James rushed into the White River.

Once on the White, float trips could make camp at Camp Thomas on the north bank or Kimberling Park on the south bank at the Kimberling crossing. Downstream were Log Way Bluff, Tibbetts Ferry and Indian Creek Spring. Many float trips traveling down the White concluded at Acacia Club or Branson on Lake Taneycomo.

Although less developed, similar camps existed on the upper White and the Kings River. Anglers could put in at Lost Bridge (now under Beaver Lake) and float down to Beaver Town, Stubblefields or Eagle Rock. Camp Calloway built around 1915 was at the confluence of the Kings and White on Epperly Bluff. Two Rivers Camp owned by V.L. Erard was located near Lost Hill at the mouth of the Kings. This camp was destroyed when the lake rose in 1957. No other known permanent camps on the Kings have been discovered by this writer, but it is clear that the Kings was frequently floated. Many suitable sites for temporary camps existed on the Kings before Table Rock Lake including Prentice, Garrison and Viola Fords and the spring at Couch Bend.

The following section is written in first person as I feel it best describes this experience.

It was a clear, warm day in February as I drove down Blunk Road just west of Galena to meet with Gary Benham. Gary has lived in Galena throughout his life. He operated a campground on the James in Galena and outfitted float trips through James River Outfitters. Gary's father and grandfather both guided float trips on the James in their time.

Gary welcomed me to his home on the high bluff overlooking Sweet Water Bottoms. The view looks out over a long straight stretch of the river. Off to the north, the James splits around an island. To the east, large sycamores with bare, white trunks line the river bank. The bottomlands are wide across the river with pasture slowly rising up to forested ridgelines. Off to the south, a bald eagle perches in its aerie, apparently protecting an egg or two. Below Gary's home on the cliff above the water lies Gentry cave, a labyrinth of passages and tunnels, snaking through the bluff.

We drove to town and picked up Buster Tilden. Buster was one of the last surviving original float guides of this area. He guided johnboats on the James and other rivers of the Table Rock area starting in the 1930's. At 91, Buster was quick of step and quick of mind. He climbed the riverbanks with two fellows half his age all afternoon and told stories the whole time. Buster knew the outfitters and the guides during the heyday of float fishing. He knew Charlie Barnes, Tom Yocum, Rollie Blunk, George Foster and Little Hoss Jennings. He floated, fished and camped with the best.

My goal for the day was to visit some of the old fishing camps on the James. I couldn't have chosen a better pair to guide me. These camps are all either on or require access through private property. Through his outfitting business, his knowledge of the area and local residents, and his personable manner, Gary could gain access to these camps. And Buster knew the stories about what these camps were like decades before.

Our first stop was at Camp Echo about 4½ river miles above Galena. The camp is reached through a well-manicured horse ranch. Camp Echo was a stopping point and campsite. It never included cabins or amenities. The camp is on a peaceful bench with the James flowing serenely beneath an attractive white bluff on the eastern shore. There is an old well with a working hand pump on the site.

About a mile and a half downstream is Camp Yocum, reached by a decent county road with the final private portion a narrow dirt trail. Camp Yocum was run by Tom Yocum and his family for many years. Buster remembered Tom as a knowledgeable guide with meticulous camp habits. Buster said Tom Yocum would allow other guides to prepare meals, but he insisted on cleaning and carefully stowing the cooking gear.

Camp Yocum was a popular camp with a lodge and several cabins for long-term stays. Surprisingly, almost all these structures are still standing and some are still used. Gary Benham lived in one of the units for a while. These wood-frame buildings have survived weather and floods for over seventy-five years. The camp is situated on a very level terrace about ten feet above the river. Hickory, oak and ash trees dot the shady bench. Buster reported that the river stretch past Yocum was a good hole for goggle-eye when Galena was the "Float Fishing Capital of the World".

The next camp we visited was Limberlost. I found Limberlost a sad place. Too close to town, the camp shows considerable intrusion by people who don't appreciate the history or natural beauty of this site. Limberlost once included a substantial lodge and cabins. The camp served as a fishing camp, vacation resort and community event venue. Gary and Ellen Benham were married at the lodge before it was destroyed by fire. Buster thought this was also the site of a ferry many years ago. All that remains now of the camp are some concrete foundation walls huddled against the hill slope. The river takes two attitudes here. A portion of the water eases into a shallow slough seeming to resign itself to stagnation. The rest of the river courses through a narrow chute, impatient to leave this place and find a more wild setting.

After leaving Limberlost behind, my guides took me past Bill Rogers Motel. The facility was still operated as a motel until recently. Bill Rogers ran a resort and fishing camp at the Kimberling Bridge for many years before moving his service to Galena when Table Rock came in. Rogers' motel and restaurant was a nexus of float fishing activity during the last years of the great float era. Gary Benham and Buster Tilden both remembered a long line of johnboats that Rogers and other outfitters kept tied up on the James just below Rogers Motel. The original Bill Rogers Motel sign still stands, but stares blindly at the concrete piers of the old wagon bridge that once crossed the river here.

Next, back down Blunk Road past the old remains of Rollie Blunk's house. It has been gone so long now, even my companions were unsure if this was the location for Arnold's Lodge. To me it didn't seem quite right. So we headed down to the river and drove right into the river bed and four-wheeled across the reasonably flat bedrock. Gary said this route was the old roadway along the river. He remembered the school bus using this path that ran several hundred yards before rising back up out of the valley. We drove as far as possible over the rock and then proceeded on foot. The dry portion of the river bed was pocked with potholes and littered with small, colorful periwinkle shells. There were no mussel shells to be seen.

We walked back up the river bank, through cane and briars, back into the forest. Soon we came across an old dam at the mouth of a small hidden stream known as Medical Spring Hollow. The dam was well-built and well-designed, still in reasonably good condition. Gravel pushed down the hollow had completely filled the streambed behind the dam, but a small flow issued from a conduit at the base of the dam and formed a small, clear pool. Buster said this was the site of Camp Care-away and I believe it was. But I now believe that this was also the site of Arnold's Lodge which was later converted into Camp Care-away. The description of Camp Arnold just fit this location too well.

Camp Care-away was opened by a wealthy oil man from Oklahoma as a summer camp for disadvantaged youth. Buster said the man was known locally as "Millionaire Jones". Some maps identify this site as Jones Camp which may help explain its history or deepen its mystery.

Whichever, there are plenty of indications that a camp existed here. Above the dam, the creek banks are lined by stone walls. Buster said the dam and walls created a swimming pool. Farther up the hollow, there are substantial piers on either side, which Buster stated supported a dining hall suspended over the small stream. Scattered around the area were footings, foundations and partial walls indicating the locations of cabins. One particularly large foundation outline was the auditorium or main hall at Camp Care-away, Buster believed.

As we stood among these ruins, we looked out across the James, wider and deeper here, even under drought conditions. Buster pointed downstream. "Just around the bend was Tilden Hole," he said. He explained that this was one of many named holes along the river that the float guides used to identify locations for fishing and camping. The Tilden family had homesteaded land across the river in the 1800's. Buster recalled plowing 200 acres of bottomland behind a brace of mules on this property as a youth. This section of the river carries his family name.

We visited one last camp that winter day- Long Camp. Gary guided us down a long gravel road that followed a steep, narrow hollow steadily down over a mile toward the river. We came out on a wide bottomland terrace. It was quiet. There was only one structure visible in the wide expanse up and down the valley- an old hand-hewn log cabin. Buster believed it was part of the old Long homestead.

To me, this site spoke volumes without saying a word. History seemed to exude from the ground. Tales of hard scrabble farming, of hearty meals in an old log cabin, of weary fishermen telling tales around a campfire. I could picture George Foster, veteran float guide, cooking pancakes over an open fire. Buster recalled George was a southpaw and his fellow floaters would sometimes request a left-handed flapjack. George's reply would be, "They come in pairs, I don't make just one."

The river flows north here, up against a high, steep, white rock bluff dotted with red cedars. Across the stream, a large section of rock ledge had fractured and fallen into the water. Both Gary and Buster thought it was a recent collapse. The James seemed to forsake itself here at Long Camp. Backwater from Table Rock Lake comes up river this far. It's not really a river anymore.

As the sun settled in the west, my companions and I headed out of the valley and back to Galena. You can still float, fish and camp at some of these sites. But remember what came before. Men like Buster Tilden ran these waters decades ago and helped develop these camps. Men like Gary Benham can still guide you to these sites and introduce you to the beauty and enjoyment of the river.

Camp Echo today

Gary Benham and Buster Tilden at Camp Yocum

White Rock Bluff from Camp Yocum

The James from the site of Camp Limberlost today

The dam at Camp Care-away

The site of Long Camp today

Cabin at the site of Long Camp

Although there are still serious anglers floating the tributaries of Table Rock, the big lakes changed the float business forever.

The streams have changed from erosion, siltation and pollution. Most outfitters today use aluminum canoes and cater to large groups of young people, youth groups and organized parties. The partying drifters far outnumber the fishermen.

George Foster, well-known float guide on the James, penned the following poem as his way of saying goodbye to the river he had loved for so long:

" *I am just an old broke down river rat, Have a story I want to tell,*
How they're fixin' to ruin our beautiful stream I tell you folks it's h__ l!
Now, you can take old Mother Nature, She has done her work with care,
Then take man's beautiful pictures, You see it's nothing to compare.
I know this old river like a book, Almost to every rock and tree,
But I have been floating it for forty odd years, you see.
Many and many a night I have camped on her nice clean gravel bars,
Sleeping out in the wide open spaces beneath the bright shining stars.
So come all you good fishers, and float while you may,
I hope to see you at Camp Rock Haven, at the Fishermen's Hat Cafe! "

Now when crossing the lake, travelers use modern steel and concrete bridges. Boaters on Table Rock can moor at well-stocked marinas, stop at lakeside restaurants and spend the night at well-appointed lake resorts. Campgrounds are park-like with electricity and running water.

The fords, ferries and camps of the White River Valley are now bridges and resorts- still the places where people and water meet.

Chapter 6
Roads, Bridges and Railroads

Long before man entered the upper White River Valley, animals created game trails through the forests, glades and stream bottoms. When Native Americans came to the area, they followed these paths and created hunting trails. Early settlers first came to this wilderness on the rivers and following the hunting trails. Wagon roads developed between settlements. Major early roads connecting developing regions surrounding the Ozarks crossed the White River valley through difficult terrain.

One of the earliest north-south thoroughfares was the Wilderness Road. The idea for a Wilderness Trail running from Springfield to Berryville was formulated by Nathaniel Kimberling and Joseph Philibert prior to the Civil War. Both men were prominent businessmen in the White River area and foresaw the need for a useful means of transportation to the coming railroad in Springfield.

They began surveying a route across the prairies on the northern and southern extremes and along the ridgetops surrounding the river valley. The Civil War delayed development of the route.

After the war, Philibert and Nathaniel's son, William Wesley Kimberling, hired war veterans to continue work on the road. Eventually, they blazed a difficult but useable road that ran from Springfield (along present-day Campbell Street) south to Dutch Store, Highlandville, Spokane and Reeds Spring. This portion of the road roughly followed present-day Highway 160. The Wilderness Road ran through Linchpin, near present-day Branson West, along the approximate route of Hwy. 13, descended into the river valley and crossed the White River at the Mayberry Ferry and continued south to Berryville. (The name Linchpin probably refers to the metal pins used on wagons. A linchpin was used to retain wheels on their axle. Many team-drawn wagons traveled along the Wilderness Road and the teamsters would often stop for repairs and rest at this location on the highland above the Kimberling Crossing at White River.)

Another wagon road ran from Reeds Spring southeast to cross the White at Boston Ferry near Forsyth. This route was known as the "Big Road" and connected to Harrison, Arkansas.

The Butterfield Stage Line operated the Overland Mail route through the Ozarks from 1858 to 1861. This stagecoach service originated in Tipton, Missouri, followed the Wire Road from Springfield to Fayetteville, Arkansas and eventually rolled all the way to San Francisco.

Stagecoach and mail service on this 2800 mile route was authorized by Congress in 1857. The contract for operating the service was awarded by Postmaster General Aaron Brown to John Butterfield. Butterfield developed an extensive transportation system consisting of 141 station stops, 250 stagecoaches, 1200 horses and the personnel and supplies to support the line.

Butterfield's mandate was to establish a service that could travel between Tipton (the western terminus of the railroad) and San Francisco in 25 days. The coaches were required to carry passengers, goods and mail. The Butterfield Line purchased Concord Coaches to service most of the route. Concord Stagecoaches were well-built wooden vehicles painted red or green with yellow running gear and leather-strap suspensions which afforded a comfortable ride.

After leaving Springfield, coaches would stop at the home of John A. Ray to pick up mail. This site would later play a prominent role in the Civil War battle at Wilson's Creek. The first official stop, sixteen miles south of Springfield, was at a station operated by John Ashmore. The next way-station was run by John Smith seven miles west of Crane. The route followed Flat Creek through Cassville with the last Missouri stop one mile south of Washburn. The first mail stop in Arkansas was at the Elk Horn Tavern, a popular rest-stop that would later become well-known during the Battle of Pea Ridge.

The Butterfield Line only ran the Overland Mail route for two and a half years. By early 1861, political unrest preceding the Civil War prompted Congress to order the route changed from its southern course to a central route from St. Joseph to Sacramento.

During its short life, the Butterfield Line provided transportation, mail delivery and access to goods for the people of the upper White River Valley. One can imagine the excitement local settlers felt when a brightly painted Butterfield Stagecoach rumbled into a local way-station, carrying passengers and mail. The Butterfield Route was a precursor to many efforts to establish reliable transportation in this rugged area.

With increased agriculture, farm-to-market roads developed throughout the area that would become Table Rock. These roads, although often little more than wagon trails, were critical to the local economy. Area residents needed efficient ways to move their farm produce to town and have access to manufactured goods.

The Old Trail

The Lakeside Drive Way

In many ways, the river and streams of this area were barriers to transportation. Where roads met the water, fords or ferries were necessary. In many places fords were simply wide spots in the stream with relatively shallow water and a firm bottom. Where the water was too deep, ferries were used. At high water levels, fords and most ferries were unusable.

In the early settlement period, the upper White River was used to transport people and goods, but it was never reliable on a large scale. Steamboats and flatboats plied the river from the early 1800's. According to Goodspeed's *1888 History of Barry County*,[39] "In 1851-52 the county granted some money to be expended on improving the navigation of White River... During the session of the Legislature in 1854-55 a bill was introduced by Senator John Gullet from this district, the title of which was 'A Bill for the Improvement of the Navigation of White River' asking an appropriation of $10,000 out of the state treasury... that sum was expended on said river." These efforts were only partially successful. Steamboats often traveled up the White as far as Forsyth. The farthest point ever reached up the river was the mouth of the James attained by the steamboat Ray in 1859.

157

The dangers of navigating the White are illustrated in the following story from *Bright Glowed My Hills* by Douglas Mahnkey :[40]

" *'Look sharp at any man who recommends hisself too highly,' the old river raftsman remarked to me one day.*

I recollect one time years ago we had a big raft of logs on the lower White River during a high rise in early spring. Most of us was experienced in rafting but was surely worried about them Wild Cat Shoals. We knew they would be rough, with wild white water rushin' over them big boulders 'neath that high bluff. Afore we got within a mile of the shoals, we could hear the roar of the flood waters on the rocks. Now, sonny, you probably don't know how a raft is operated, but we have thousands of logs held together in sections with boards and planks nailed on the logs to hold them together. The crew poles the raft along the river, floatin' with the current, keepin' it pushed away from treacherous spots and the river banks. A man in front directs the operations and a good man on the back of the raft handles the sweep. The sweep is a long pole that is in the water. The man with the sweep can guide or steer the raft by strokes with this sweep. The man in front, who is the pilot, calls out his orders above the roar of the water so the man steerin' the raft will know whether to sweep to the left or the right. None of us felt capable of pilotin' this big raft over the Wild Cat Shoals since the water was so high and wild. We beached the raft and tied her up about a mile above the shoals. We began to make inquiry at the little settlement for a pilot who could run us safely over the Wild Cat. A feller came forward and volunteered that he was 'the best damn pilot on the White' and for $5.00- which was a lot of money in those days- he'd pilot us over the shoals, safe and sound. He continued to boast and brag about his pilotin' ability. Well, we hired him and he took his place on the front of the raft as we shoved her off into the whirlin' stream. We put two strong men on the sweep and hoped for the best. That water was deep and cold as ice, and we weren't wantin' a bath that cold spring day, for sure. The raft rushed on and on, and our new pilot, standin' proud and straight, began to give his orders, loud and clear as the raft neared the shoals.

'Give her half a stroke to the left,' and the men at the sweep obeyed.

'Now about a half stroke to the right,' and it was done, and

*the speed of the raft increased and the huge rocks with the white
water rushin' around and over them were just ahead.*

*The pilot roared, 'Give her a full stroke to the right! Another
full stoke to the right!' Louder and louder roared the water and
faster and faster rushed our raft.*

*Our pilot was now frantic as he yelled, 'Give her a full
stroke to the left! Another full stroke to the left! Give her hell to
the left!'*

*And just then our raft piled onto the great rocks, breakin'
into pieces and spillin' men and supplies into the cold, wild
water. We all reached the shore without the loss of a man, but it
seemed a miracle. So you see, sonny, never put too much trust in
a man who recommends hisself too highly."*

With the advent of the automobile, roads were improved and
new ones were built. (Author's note: Road names and locations
were changed many times in this area, particularly just preceding
and during construction of Table Rock. The author has attempted
to document these changes wherever possible.) By the 1940's,
several major routes crisscrossed the upper White region. The
major north-south road was State Highway 13 (earlier 43). State
Highway 86 was the predominant east-west route. Just before
Table Rock was built, the only paved routes in the area were
Hwy. 13 and portions of 86 and 148. The remaining roads were
gravel or graded dirt.

Highway 43 ran from Springfield to Arkansas roughly
following the Wilderness Road route from Reeds Spring south.
This road, paved by the early 1940's as Hwy. 13, crossed the
James River at Galena and the White at the Kimberling crossing.
A wagon bridge built in 1915 carried traffic across the James
at Galena. This span was replaced by the Y-bridge in 1927. The
Y-bridge crossed the river as a single span and then branched
off into two separate sections, one heading north on then 44 and
the other continuing south on 43. The bridge has been closed to
traffic since 1986, but still stands and is on the National Register
of Historic Places.

View of the road across from Camp Rock Haven site c.1956

Highway 43 crossed the White via the Kimberling Ferry until the White River Bridge was built in 1922. This bridge was washed out and rebuilt twice. With the coming of the Table Rock Project, the new Kimberling Bridge was constructed. At 1900 feet, it is the longest bridge over Table Rock Lake. During construction of the lake, the old bridge was sold for scrap. However, the flood of 1957 inundated the bridge and most of it was never removed. Today, the old bridge still stands, one hundred feet below the lake's surface.

Twice during construction of Table Rock, ferries were used at the Hwy. 13 crossing. From May to September of 1957, massive flooding raised the water to 895 feet. The old bridge was inundated and the new bridge was incomplete. Army personnel from Ft. Wood set up a two ferry operation at this site for essential traffic. One of the ferries was called the "Happy Bob". Tragically, one soldier drowned during this operation. Again in the spring of 1958, premature flooding of the lake necessitated a ferry at Hwy. 13.

Old Highway 86, developed in 1933, crossed what would become Table Rock Lake in three places. From US 65 south of Branson, the road entered the river valley at Jakes Branch.

The old road still exists here as a boat launch. Highway 86 crossed Long Creek and exited the valley where Old Hwy. 86 Park exists today. The route continued as a paved road up 13 to Lampe where it became a gravel road crossing Big Indian Creek on a bridge at Baxter. Hwy. 86 then proceeded on the present route of H and 39 to the old bridge at Shell Knob. This portion of the highway entered what is today the lake at Twin Rivers, ran around Lost Hill and crossed the White on the Shell Knob Bridge at the mouth of the Kings. It then proceeded up Needle's Eye to Shell Knob and on to Cassville.

The first White River Bridge at the confluence of the Kings and White Rivers was constructed by Gillioz Construction Co. of Monett, Mo. The bridges at Shell Knob and Mano were realized through a Barry County road and bridge levy approved in 1927.

Originally, there were no plans for a new bridge to cross the lake at Shell Knob. Pleas from the citizens of Shell Knob, Viola and the surrounding area and the support of Senator Stuart Symington and Congressman Charley Brown convinced the Corps of Engineers to add the new bridge late in the project process.

There was a period when the new bridge was incomplete and the old bridge was inundated. By the time the new Shell Knob Bridge was ready for traffic, the old bridge was permanently covered by the lake. In the fall of 1959, demolition was carried out by divers who used underwater torches to cut the girders and set dynamite to blast out the piers. It was reported that thousands of fish were killed by the detonation. Rubble from this bridge is still below the surface between Needle's Eye and Lost Hill Island.

The new bridges over Table Rock Lake were primarily built by construction firms under contract to the state. The Central Crossing Bridge at Shell Knob was one of the last constructed.

This span was built by Rallo Construction of St. Louis starting in 1957, under the inspection of the State of Missouri.

Duke Sherfy, an employee of Rallo Construction, worked as an equipment operator and labor foreman on this project. Duke described the following construction sequence. After surveying an acceptable crossing, the White River was diverted by temporary weir dams and access berms were constructed out into the river. At the location for each pier, forms were constructed and footings were excavated up to 78 feet into the river bedrock. Most of this work was performed by hand operated air jacks while pumps removed the water from the pits. Concrete was then poured to form the footings.

The piers were formed of highly reinforced concrete poured in sections. Moveable forms were used to allow a nearly continuous pour of a gravel, sand, cement and water mix. All gravel and sand were trucked to the site from a Berryville quarry. The concrete was mixed at a concrete plant constructed at the bridge site. Concrete was moved to the pouring location on a cable-way system. A large tower was built on each side of the river, perfectly aligned with the bridge span. A bucket skiff suspended from the cable-way traveled between the towers. The skiff, used to transport men, concrete, steel and other materials, was operated by the "bellboy" in the skiff and the cable-way operator on shore. These two men communicated by walkie-talkie.

Each pier was poured to a certain height and then "capped" with a block. The next slightly smaller section was then poured on top of the cap. Steel "rockers" were attached to the top of the main piers and "sliders" on the two smaller end piers. These members provided support and allowed movement of the bridge superstructure. The bridge was built from pre-fabricated steel beams bolted and hot riveted in place. All steel was sandblasted and painted.

The roadbed was poured in place on hanging forms. The bridge floor was asphalted and road approaches completed. Missouri constructed a re-routed highway 39 across the bridge.

Projects like the Central Crossing Bridge provided employment for many local men. Those hired to work on this bridge joined the union and were paid $1.90 an hour. Although a good wage at the time, this was very difficult and dangerous work. Duke Sherfy relates a story of a terrible fire that occurred during the building of Shell Knob's new bridge.

While pouring pier #3, five men including Duke were inside the forms on Christmas Day repairing the protective tarps. It was necessary to keep the fresh concrete warm using the tarps and propane heaters to assure proper curing. A fire occurred burning all five men seriously. One later died as a result of his injuries. Duke reported one other man died during bridge construction from a fall.

It should be remembered that the beautiful lake, dam, bridges and roads of Table Rock that we enjoy today were the result of the blood, sweat and tears of many hard-working people. Some even gave their lives on this project.

Highway 76 was originally constructed in 1914 by the cooperative road districts of Stone and Taney Counties. It was a rough unpaved route following the undulating terrain between Branson and Reeds Spring. Roads like this were built by hand with the aid of mules and horses. County road commissions required able-bodied men over 21 to work two to four days a year to work off their poll tax, providing much of the labor for road construction. Hwy. 76 was upgraded to a paved road before Table Rock was constructed, but like most area roads followed a different route from its present course. At the time of construction of the lake, 76 ran along the farther north route of present-day 160 from Rockaway Beach to Reeds Spring. Today's Hwy. 76 follows what was 148 when Table Rock was developed.

There were many other roads that crossed the White and its tributaries prior to Table Rock's development. Few of these roads were paved, but they still provided access between communities and served as farm-to-market routes. Loss of these roads and their associated bridges were of major concern to local residents. Only four major bridges were originally planned for the lake. Access to transportation was critical to the local economies. After completion of the lake, areas without a bridge could become very isolated.

The Corps of Engineers, the states of Missouri and Arkansas, area counties and towns and the local citizens all had conflicting ideas on how the development of roads and bridges should proceed on the Table Rock Project. Most of the major road re-routing was done by the states with some support from counties.

The Federal government had the right to flood all the bridges, but the state or county retained ownership of them. The state estimated that removal of the major bridges would be more costly than salvaging them. Some were sold as scrap and fully or partially removed, but many were left in place. Eventually, all the major bridges, except at the Kimberling crossing, were demolished, due primarily to their hazard to navigation on the future lake.

In addition to the Kimberling and Central Crossing bridges, major spans were built at Long Creek, Cape Fair and Eagle Rock. The Long Creek Bridge was constructed along a re-routed Hwy. 86. Cape Fair's old bridge crossing the James on Hwy. 148 was demolished. Portions of the old approach pylons are still visible along the shoreline just south of the new bridge. Gary H. James Construction Company of Oklahoma City built the new Cape Fair Bridge and 1.4 miles of approach.

The Farwell Bridge crossing the White at Eagle Rock on Route P was removed and replaced by the new span on the newly routed 86. The original Farwell Bridge was constructed by J.C. Ault of Cassville in 1937. The new 772 feet bridge was built by James Construction Co. and included 1.35 miles of road relocation. The old road bed and portions of the bridge abutments can be seen just below the water on the east side of the Eagle Rock Bridge. After crossing the White, Route P proceeded to Eagle Rock where it spanned Roaring River.

Many smaller river and creek crossings were permanently lost to Table Rock. The remnants of these crossings now exist only as rubble at the lake's edge or shadowy fragments on the lake bottom. The old roadbeds have become migration routes for the fishes.

Route E ran north from Cape Fair and bridged Flat Creek. This bridge was removed and replaced with a new structure at the same location on 173. Portions of the old bridge's accesses can be seen below the new span.

A major farm-to-market road (now 39-1) traveled from Shell Knob east. This gravel road crossed the White on Townsend Bridge at Philibert Bluff and then connected to 86. The Townsend Bridge was destroyed by floods prior to Table Rock's development.

Before the big reservoir was built, State Highway 39 ran from the Arkansas State line, through Golden and crossed the White near present-day Big M. The bridge at this location was built by M.E. Gillioz Construction Co. of Monett in 1929 through a county road and bridge levy. The road passed through Mano and continued north to 86. The bridge at Mano was removed and not replaced. The old Hwy. 39 roadbed swings around the small peninsula at Big M Park and crosses the marina cove. County Road F traveled from Hwy. 39 just north of Mano to Roaring River, crossing Rock Creek on a small bridge. Mano and Golden became more isolated without a through-route. Although they did not develop more as towns, the lake did bring extensive progress in the form of lakeshore homes to these areas.

A new bridge was constructed at Enon crossing Yocum Creek just above Long Creek. The span was 300 feet long and consisted of concrete piers, steel stringers and a wooden floor. The new bridge was constructed by Griffith & Beadell Construction Co. of Merriam, Ks. and cost $130,000. The bridge replaced a low-water crossing and required the relocation of 3500 feet of county road. This location has recently received a new two-lane concrete bridge over Yocum Creek.

An unimproved road (once called the James River Road) started at Hwy. 13 just north of the Kimberling Bridge and crossed the James on a bridge just below Joe Bald. This bridge consisting of steel girders, concrete pilings and a wooden deck was washed out by high water in 1956 and not replaced. The road proceeded north, crossing the James again at Oswalt Ford and ran up Aunts Creek. Where this old road first crossed the James was the site of the original Philibert homestead.

The original Philibert homestead was established along the ridge and terraces just north of the James and White intersection. After crossing the James, the road followed the ridge through the Philibert property. This area consisted of large tracts of river bottomland, terraces and a high ridge running from the northwest toward the southeast. The Loftin farm had several structures near the end of this ridge.

Bridge at Loftin's

Wagon Bridge Over Lake Taneycomo

The bridges at Holiday Island- Note the center section of the old bridge removed.

The Golden Gate Bridge at Beaver Town

The old Shell Knob Bridge

The bridges at Kimberling City

The new bridge over Flat Creek at Cape Fair viewed past the old bridge abutments

The bridge abutments at the James River Bridge at Cape Fair washed out by a flood about 1940. The man in the photo is believed to be the local postman attempting to deliver the mail.

Railroads

The upper White River Valley presented an extraordinary challenge to the railroads. The extremely rugged hills and valleys and the unbridled streams were difficult barriers to the construction of rails. Building mountain railroads was expensive and dangerous.

The North Arkansas Railroad from Seligman to Eureka Springs was constructed in the 1880's, primarily to carry passengers. A train ride during this period was exciting and dangerous. The roadbeds did not use ballast and ties were hand cut. The rail cars were made of wood and used wood stoves for heat and kerosene or oil lamps for light. Derailments frequently resulted in fires.

The North Arkansas crossed the White River at Beaver Town. The tracks cut through Narrows Bluff on the neck of land between the White River and Leatherwood Creek. The railroad followed Leatherwood Creek on into Eureka Springs.

The railroad bridge at Beaver was used until the rail line discontinued service in 1961. For a time in the 1970-80's, the track was reopened and used as an excursion line from Eureka Springs. The rails were last removed from this section around 1987. Today, the piers for the bridge provide a backdrop for swimmers at Beaver Park.

The White River Division of the Missouri Pacific Railroad completed tracks from Joplin to Newport, Arkansas in the early 20th century. The building of this railway was a monumental task. The line consisted of several tunnels, bridges, trestles, steep grades and tight curves.

The White River Railroad crossed the James River at Galena on a bridge constructed in 1904. The tracks crossed the White at Branson. Both these railroad bridges exist today and are still used.

The railroad bridge at Beaver today- Note the cut in the narrows.

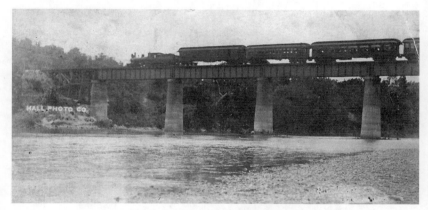

The White River Railroad Bridge Branson

Reeds Spring Railroad Tunnel

The upper White River Valley has always been a challenge to transportation. Many of the earliest inhabitants used the river as a dangerous means of travel. Over time, rough trails and wagon roads were carved through the hills. Many of these trails are still the basic route of today's present highways. Crossing the rivers and streams occurred on foot and by boat, then by ferries and in the 20th century, bridges were built at many sites. With the coming of Table Rock Lake, the roads and bridges of the area were significantly changed and improved. While driving over one of today's lake bridges, one can only imagine the difficulty of traversing the rough terrain and flowing rivers before the big lake came.

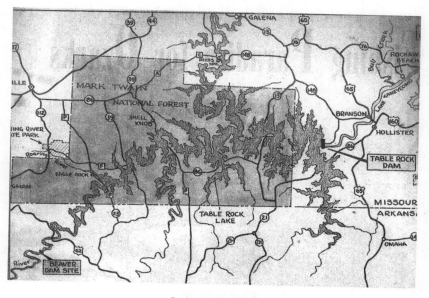

Lake map 1956

Chapter 7
Diving Sites

Most of the recreational diving sites on Table Rock Lake are downstream from Kimberling City. The lower end of the lake has the clearest water and this is where several popular diving destinations exist. Some of the sites are natural features; others are man-made. Most of the sunken boats were purposely scuttled to provide interesting diving.

Duck Island is located off State Park. There is a 25 foot cruiser sunk in 45 feet of water on the east side. Two miles south of Duck Island is Breezy Point, the Saddle and Breezy Island. The location is an interesting natural feature in a bend of the original Long Creek streambed. A steep, narrow ridge runs underwater out from the west shore and then rises to form Breezy Island.

Farther up Long Creek is a deep dive on the flooded town of Oasis. In over 100 feet of water lie the remains of the quaint little town- the one-lane bridge, foundations and building rubble. Most of Oasis was destroyed in the flood of 1957, including the large mill. The deterioration caused by being under water for 60 years has left little remaining of the settlement.

In the large cove north of Table Rock Dam lies the Enchanted Forest. This is a popular site known for its breathtaking visual effect of sunlight shining down through a large grove of submerged hardwood trees. There are often many fish in the area.

In Jacques Creek lies a wreck site known as the Zebulon Pike. The Zebulon Pike operated as an excursion boat on Table Rock Lake for several years. It eventually was moored in Jacques Creek alongside its boarding barge, The General. Later, the Pike was moved and kept at Long Creek Marina. The barge was scuttled in about 90 feet of water in Jacques creating an exciting dive site. The Zebulon Pike was purchased by Bass Pro Shop and is now dry docked in Nixa. Just south of the Zebulon Pike site is Jake's Point Island. This small island has a large cabin cruiser sunk on its southwest side.

Two other sunken boats lie on the lake floor downstream from the Kimberling Bridge. At Point 7, there is a 40 foot cruiser in 65 feet of water and between Points 6 and 7 there is a sunken houseboat at a depth of 45 feet.

In the small cove on the northeast side of the Kimberling Bridge is a small boat sunk in about 40 feet. The old Kimberling Bridge is mostly intact almost directly below the new bridge, 175 feet below Table Rock's surface. This is a deep dive, only safe for well-trained technical divers, that provides an interesting viewpoint on what was buried by Table Rock Lake.

These are some of the sites which reveal the types of things covered by the lake. All diving requires special training and equipment, particularly deep dives. People interested in seeing these underwater treasures should seek the assistance of a diving guide service.

Epilogue

If you compare the way of life in these hills between about 1940 and 1960, you see a dramatic shift. In 1940, the upper White River Valley was almost completely an agrarian-based economy. There was little or no electricity or telephone service and most roads were very rough. Contact with the outside world was primarily through radio, newspapers and visitors to the area. By 1960, tourism was becoming a very big part of the local economy. REA had brought electrical service to most of the region and telephones were widely used. The transportation infrastructure had been greatly improved.

The author has nothing but respect for this Ozark culture. Life in this region before World War II was difficult, but also full of beauty and joy. What Table Rock Lake brought to this area was disliked by some and appreciated by others. Life was improved in many ways, but the way of life followed here for many decades was dramatically altered. As with most progress, it is difficult to see it as completely good or bad- it is just different.

Many of the changes that occurred because of Table Rock Lake would have happened sooner or later anyway. It is important to understand and appreciate what went before. I hope this small book helps shed some light on what was Buried By Table Rock Lake.

Table Rock Lake filling at Stallions Bluff

The lake covering Cole Ford on the James

Table Rock covering up the James River Bridge at Cape Fair

Table Rock Lake burying the bridge at Mash Hollow at Cape Fair

Photo Credits

Hall photos- George Edward Hall took photographs of the Ozarks from 1906 to about 1922. He lived in Branson until 1916 when he, his wife Vallie and their only child Lillian moved to Galena. Around 1922, the Halls relocated to Illinois and stopped producing photographs.

Hall reproduced many of his original photos into postcards which were sold as souvenirs. The popularity of The Shepherd of the Hills by Harold Bell Wright helped promote his photographs of this area. George Hall produced about 1,000 known photos. Many of them do a wonderful job of depicting life and activities in the Ozarks during the early 20th century.

All of Hall's photographs are in the public domain. Chloe LaRue of Reeds Spring has several original Hall postcards which she salvaged from the collection of Dr. Shumate. Mrs. LaRue was kind enough to loan her Hall photos for reproduction in this book.

The remaining Hall pictures reproduced in this book were obtained from the archived Harold Bell Wright website www.hbw.addr.com. Gerry Chudleigh (now deceased) did a fine job of collecting and displaying these photographs on his website.

Reference Bibliography

Corps of Engineers, U.S. Army Little Rock District, <u>Table Rock Reservoir and How the U.S. Buys It</u>, 1955

Charlie Farmer, *Devil's Pool, A History of Big Cedar Lodge*, JLM Publishing Co., Springfield, Mo., 1995

Irene Horner, *Roaring River Heritage*, 1978

W.C. Jameson, *Buried Treasure of the Ozarks*, August House Publishers, 1990

Addah Langley Matthews, "Early Barry County", Barry County Historical Society, 1964

Senator Emory Melton, *Delaware Town and the Swan Trading Post 1822-1831*, Litho Printers

Senator Emory Melton, *The First 150 Years in Cassville, Missouri*, Litho Printers, 1995

Ted Sare, *Some Recollections of an Ozarks Float Trip Guide*, Webster County Printing, 1998

Phillip W. Steele, *Butterfield Run Through the Ozarks*, Heritage Publishing, 1966

Stone County Historical Society, *History of Stone County Missouri*, 1989

Frank Reuter, editor, *In the Heart of Ozark Mountain Country*, White Oak Press, 1992

Index

I

Indian Creek- 26,28,39,43,44,72,73,110, 117,127,161
Indian Creek Shelter- 43
Indian Creek Spring- 144

J

Jackson Hollow- 66,138,144
Jacksonville- 23
Jacques Creek- 110,174
Jacques Point Island- 110
Jacques Creek Cemetery- 89
Jake's Point Island- 174
Jakie archaeologic site- 35-37,45-48
Jakie Branch- 46
Jakie Hollow- 45
James River- 9, 17, 18, 30, 31, 37, 53, 57, 61, 65 - 69,94,103,105,110,126,143,15 9,165,169,170,178
James River Road- 165
James, Jesse- 54,76,78
Jamestown- 17,18,30
jellyfish- 93
Jennings, Little Hoss- 71,145
Joe Bald- 9,69,71,78,116,144,165
John Moore Road- 74,76
Johnson Cemetery- 88,89
Jones Camp- 147
Jones, Joy L.- 17,103,104
Jones-Wolf, Winnie Bee- 6

K

karst- 92,113
Kimball Shelter- 45
Kimberling Bridge- 9-11 13, 42, 127, 131, 134, 139, 146, 159, 160, 164, 165, 168, 174, 175
Kimberling City, Mo.- 13,111,127
Kimberling Ferry- 10, 12, 13, 115, 126, 155, 160
Kimberling Park- 11,144
Kimberling, Nathaniel- 154
Kimberling, William Wesley- 10,127,154
Kings River- 21,23,24,26,36,39,45,49,53, 79,98,107,108,118,125,127,129,134,1 37,144,161
Knob Hill Acres- 24,129

L

Lampe, Mo.- 25,26,28,43,76,78,161
land appraisal- 51,90
land clearing- 52,99

Lander archaeologic site- 36,43
Leatherwood Creek- 108,109,170
Leland, John- 21
Lewellyn archaeologic site- 41
Lewis Ford- 54,75,126,127
Limberlost- 143,146,151
Linchpin, Mo.- 154
Loftin archaeologic site- 36,37,42,110
Loftin, Ben- 68-71,165,166
Loftis, Tim- 129-131
Log Cabin Camp- 144
Logslide Bluff- 97
Long Bottoms- 105
Long Camp- 143,148,152
Long Creek- 3, 5, 6, 9, 32, 33, 41, 85, 109, 111, 125, 126,161,174
Long Creek Bridge- 164,165
Look Out Point- 43
Lost Hill Island- 23,108,144,161

M

Magers Cave- 42,43,113
Mahnkey, C.P.- 6,8
Mahnkey, Douglas- 3,8,158
Mahnkey, Mary Elizabeth- 6-9
Mano, Mo.- 161,165
Marionville, Mo.- 64
Mark Twain National Forest- 52,99,122
Marvel Cave- 71,73,114,115,140
Mash Hollow- 144,178
Massey, Ellen Gray- 5
Mayberry- 10,127,154
Maybry- see Mayberry
McCullough School- 27
McCullough, Edna Hazel- 26
McFarland archaeologic site- 41
McKee family- 26,79-81,83
Medical Spring Hollow- 147
medicine woman- 45-47
Midwife- 86,87
Mill Creek- 23,39,44,81,82,84,108,114
Missouri & North Arkansas Railroad- 14,15,108,170,171
Missouri Archaeological Society- 37, 38, 40, 46, 47
Missouri Pacific Railroad- 32,170
Moon Song- 104-106
Morris Cemetery- 89
Morris Ford/Ferry- 23,24,126,127,129
Mud Cave- 73
mussels- 39,44,49,93,94,147

185

Endnotes

1. Mahnkey, Douglas, "Oasis on Long Creek", <u>Ozark Mountaineer</u>, September 1972
2. Gray Massey, Ellen, *A Candle Within Her Soul Mary Elizabeth Mahnkey and Her Ozarks (1877-1948)*, Bittersweet, Inc., 1996
3. Ibid
4. Ibid
5. Rayburn, Otto Ernest, <u>Forty Years in the Ozarks,</u> Ozark Guide Press, Eureka Springs, Arkansas, 1957
6. Ibid
7. Table Rock Reservoir map, U.S. Engineer Office, Little Rock, Arkansas, December, 1944
8. Long, Kathryn, Stone County Historical/Geneological Society, <u>Stone County, Missouri A Pictorial History 1851-2001</u>, The Donning Company Publishers, 2001
9. Ball, Faye (Maloney) and Gaede, Darla (Ball), <u>Our Easleys,</u> 1972
10. *Springfield News & Leader,* July 15, 1956
11. Ball, Ibid
12. Ilium, Steve, <u>The Shell Knob Civilian Conservation Corps</u>
13. McCullough, Edna Hazel, "Recollections of Life in Williams Township, Stone County, Missouri", *The History of Stone County, Missouri,* Stone County Missouri Historical Society, 1989, p.15
14. Rayburn, Otto Ernest, "Ozark Guide Yearbook", 1965
15. Kimball, Stanley B., "Discovery: Nauvoo Found in Seven States", *Ensign,* April 1973
16. Schoolcraft, Henry Rowe, Journal of a Tour into the Interior of Missouri and Arkansaw, from Potosi, or Mine a Burton in Missouri territory, in a South-West Direction, toward the Rocky Mountains, Performed in the Years 1818 and 1819, London, Richard Phillips and Company, 1821
17. Kalen and Morrow, "Report for Galena, Missouri Historic Preservation Survey", Forsyth, Missouri, 1989
18. Wikipedia.org, "Dewey Jackson Short"
19. Goodspeed, <u>Goodspeed's 1889 History of Carroll</u>, The Goodspeed Publishing Co., 1889
20. Chapman, Carl and Eleanor F., *Indians and Archaeology of Missouri*, University of Missouri Press, 1964, 1983
21. Chapman, Carl, <u>The Missouri Archaeologist</u>, April-June 1956, University of Missouri
22. Adams, Lee M., *Memoir of the Missouri Archaeological Society,* December 1950
23. Adams, Lee M., <u>Archaeological Investigations of Southwestern Missouri, The Missouri Archaeoligist</u>, Vol. 20, December 1958
24. Chapman, Maxwell and Kozlovich, <u>A Preliminary Archaeologic Survey of the Table Rock Reservoir Area, Stone County Missouri</u>, The Missouri Archaeologist, October 1951
25. Chapman, Carl, editor, <u>A Report of Progress</u>, 1955-6 and Chapman, Carl, <u>Preliminary Salvage Archaeology in the Table Rock Reservoir Area, Missouri, The Missouri Archaeologist,</u> April-July 1956
26. O'Brien, Michael J. and Wood, W. Raymond, *The Prehistory of Missouri*, University of Missouri Press, 1958
27. Chapman, Carl, <u>A Resume of Table Rock Archaeologic Investigations, The Missouri Archaeologist</u>, 1956
28. Bray, Robert T., <u>The Culture-Complexes and Sequence at the Rice Site Stone County, Missouri, The Missouri Archaeologist,</u> April-July 1956
29. Chapman, Carl, editor, <u>A Report of Progress Archaeological Research by the University of Missouri</u>, 1955-6, Missouri Archaeological Society, 1957

30. Schoolcraft, Henry Rowe, *Journal of a Tour Into the Interior of Missouri and Arkansas 1818-1819*, Richard Phillips and Company, 1821

31. Ibid

32. Goodspeed, *Goodspeed's 1888 History of Barry County*, The Goodspeed Publishing Co.,1888

33. Schoolcraft, Henry Rowe, Ibid

34. Morrow, Lynn, "The Yocum Silver Dollar", White River Valley Historical Quarterly, Volume 8, Number 11, Spring 1985

35. Goodspeed, Ibid

36. Schoffelmayer, V.H., "Radium Mine in the Ozarks", *Technical World*, Vol. 18, 1913

37. Schoolcraft, Ibid

38. The Taney County Republican, September 18, 1963

39. Goodspeed, Ibid

40. Mahnkey, Douglas, *Bright Glowed My Hills*, School of the Ozarks Press, 1968